Cross
of
Valour

John Melady

Cover by Laurie McGaw

Scholastic-TAB Publications Ltd.
123 Newkirk Road, Richmond Hill, Ontario
Canada

The author gratefully acknowledges all those who have provided photographs for this book. Particular credit is given to the following: Correctional Service Canada (87, 94), Department of National Defence Canada (22, 28, 29, 32), John Evans Photo (116, 128), Glenbow Archives (59, 66, 68), Halifax Police (102), Stu LeBaron (122), Livingston Photo (9), John Melady (54), *Merritt Herald* (47), Royal Canadian Mounted Police (72, 73, 80), *The Toronto Star* (136).

Canadian Cataloguing in Publication Data

Melady, John.
    Cross of Valour

ISBN 0-590-71510-0

1. Cross of Valour — Juvenile literature.
2. Heroes — Canada — Juvenile literature.
3. Heroines — Canada — Juvenile literature.
I. Title.

CR6257.C76M44 1985   j920'.071   C85-098473-4

1st printing 1985   **Printed in Canada**

For my wife Mary

One day, three years ago, I was on a plane over the Pacific Ocean, somewhere between Tokyo and Vancouver. The flight was long and tiring and the magazine I was reading was not particularly interesting. But just as I was about to set it aside, I noticed a brief story about a man who had won the Cross of Valour, Canada's highest award for bravery. I was fascinated by what I read.

At the time, I knew almost nothing about the award, and even less about the individuals who had received it. Later on, when I learned there was almost no information available about those heroes, I decided to write this book. In the process, I feel I have come to know a truly select group of human beings.

I would like to thank several people who made my writing task easier, and who must share whatever tribute this little volume may deserve. In addition to the Cross of Valour winners themselves, and to others who are actually named in the book, I am indebted to the following: Bruce Beatty, Roy Bonisteel, Butch Boucher, David Boyd, Mary Bracey, Christopher Brooks, Captain Robert Butt, Maureen Curow, Maureen Curtis, Jim Dean, Major Al Ditter, Cliff Fielding, Robert Hughes, David John, Scott Larmon, Terry Leeder, Greg Mackenzie, Sheila Mackey, Rick Olsson, Kate Padam, Doctor Bob Patrick, Steve Rowland, Brian Salt, Dave Saunders, Arthur Schwartz, Paul Stanway, John Ward, and Joe Williams.

I also owe a special thanks to Andrée Traversy who was very helpful during my inquiries at Rideau Hall, and to Esther Parry for her editorial and word processing skills. Without those two women — who have never met — this book probably would not have been completed.

John Melady,
Trenton, Ontario,
July 23, 1985.

By the same author:

Explosion
Escape From Canada!
Korea: Canada's Forgotten War

Contents

Foreword

At 11:29 A.M., the television lights came on, the military band began to play, and the crowd fell still. One minute later, the Governor General of Canada entered the room. He moved directly to the dais, smiled at the audience, and stood at attention for *God Save the Queen*. Then, as the strains of the anthem faded, the Investiture of Canadian decorations for bravery began.

In 1972, the Government of Canada created a series of three decorations intended to recognize and honour deserving individuals who perform outstanding acts of heroism. Presented by the Governor General on behalf of the Queen, these medals are called the Cross of Valour, the Star of Courage, and the Medal of Bravery.

Always and everywhere, qualities of heroism have commanded admiration and respect. Those who risk their lives to save or protect others defy the instinct of self-preservation, and in doing so, exhibit a generosity of spirit that provides inspiration to all. It is fitting that such service and sacrifice should be acknowledged and acclaimed, and medals are a means of expressing symbolically the nation's gratitude and the high esteem in which those who receive the awards are held.

The most prestigious decoration of all, the Cross of Valour, is given for acts of the most conspicuous courage in circumstances of extreme peril. To date, only 14 people have received the award. This book tells their stories.

Anna Lang

Anna Lang of Nauwigewauk, New Brunswick, looks back at the events that led up to her winning of the Cross of Valour as if they were all part of a terrible dream, a nightmare that somehow came true, a hell so horrible she is amazed she escaped it.

At noon on Tuesday, September 9, 1980, 42-year-old Lang and her friend, 31-year-old Lana Walsh, were returning from Saint John where they had been working out in a city gymnasium. With them, in the rear seat of Anna's new red two-door Buick, was Walsh's four-year-old son Jaye. Anna was driving.

Because the day was warm, Lana had opened the window on her side of the car. The radio was on, but neither woman paid much attention to it. They were too busy chatting, discussing the events of the morning and the dangerous situation they knew existed at the Hammond River bridge, some 10 kilometres ahead.

The bridge in question is a 100-metre long, two-lane reinforced concrete structure carrying provincial Highway 1 over the Hammond River, 30 kilometres northeast of Saint John. The traffic deck of the bridge is nine metres above the water, and is supported by five massive, tapered pillars. In the late summer, only three of these supports are in the water. The river is about 80 metres wide, and in the vicinity of the overpass, two metres and more in depth. The current is not strong.

The highway approaches to the bridge are hazardous at the best of times because drivers coming from either direction must first negotiate a series of sweeping downhill curves immediately before reaching it. On this day however, the major hazard at the Hammond River involved the bridge itself. For over a week the south lane had been closed.

"They were replacing the right guardrail of the thing," recalls Anna Lang today. "I had driven over it several times when it was under construction, but it always scared me. Because one lane was closed, they had traffic lights set up at each end. The only trouble was, you could be halfway across and the lights would change and cars would start coming towards you. That happened to me one night, and I had to crowd into the construction area to let them pass. That was why I hated the bridge, and why Lana and I were talking about it as we went along. Both of us said we knew some-body would be hurt there before long. It was just too dangerous."

As the two women continued their journey, neither knew that a large gasoline truck was behind them. Although it was still out of sight, it was rapidly drawing closer. The huge 22 wheel, 50 tonne Brunswick Petroleum transport was driven by 34-year-old Charles Steeves, a trucker with 14 years of accident-free experience behind him. The tanker carried 45 000 litres of gasoline.

In the meantime, on the bridge ahead, most of the guardrail rebuilding was halted while the construction crew ate lunch. Several men had gone to their cars for sandwiches, or to the nearby Mandarin House restaurant for a hot meal. Because of the hour, only a handful of workers remained on the job. The time was 12:35 P.M.

As Anna eased her car around the long curve that leads down onto the western end of the bridge, she noticed that the temporary traffic light facing her was green. She saw no vehicles coming towards her, nor did she realize that Charles Steeves' gasoline tanker was less than 20 metres behind.

Just then, the light turned red.

"When the red came on, I automatically stopped the car," explains Lang with a shudder. "Then I looked in the rearview mirror. All I could see were two headlights and a grille. Perhaps I saw the body of the truck but I can't remember it. The grille seemed to fill my whole back window and his horn was blaring and I was screaming: 'Oh God,

Lana, he's not going to stop. He's not going to stop.'"

Up in the cab of his truck, Charles Steeves was terrified. He jammed on his brakes and sounded his horn. Yet he knew he could never stop in time. "My God," he thought to himself, "I'm going to kill them all."

The careering tanker then smashed into the back of the Lang auto, demolishing the entire rear end and ramming the trunk against the front seat. In the same instant, the back window exploded inwards and hundreds of jagged glass particles were driven into the interior of the car. Little Jaye Walsh was knocked flying into the front seat.

"When the back window popped, the glass made the inside of the car look like a cave with ice crystals hanging down," Lang recalls. "The ice kept coming until it covered the roof, the sides and even the dash. I remember being pushed forward and then crawling back to the seat again. My head hit the steering wheel and my glasses were thrown off. The whole thing seemed to be in slow motion. Everything was so slow that it's still imprinted on my mind. It was as if you were watching a movie and all these things were happening at once — but they were barely moving. Lana was thrown around as much as I was."

Walsh was tossed screaming against the windshield, shattering it. At the same time, with a mother's instinct, she grabbed Jaye and held him to her. The possibility that he would be harmed bothered her far more than the thought of injury to herself. She also knew that her husband would be devastated if anything happened to the boy.

The few remaining construction workers on the bridge were momentarily transfixed by the loud crash and it's suddenness. Near them, however, a young man named Steve Hickey, who along with his three-year-old nephew Kevin had been walking to the other side, did not even pause to see what was happening. Hickey scooped Kevin off his feet and raced with the child across the bridge and out of danger. As he did so, the onrushing car and truck, now locked together in a fatal embrace, hurtled forward in a wild cacophony of terror.

In a desperate last-second attempt to avoid hitting the car in front of him, Charles Steeves had tried to swing the behemoth he piloted to the left, into the narrow space between the Lang auto and the side of the bridge. He had failed. As his truck telescoped the car, the two vehicles ploughed through black and yellow traffic barriers and construction equipment, and finally rammed the cement forms and steel reinforcing rods with which the new guardrails would be built.

"The impact of the crash tore the tires from my car," explains Lang. "Then there was a loud, grating, grinding sound, like a teacher scratching her nails across a blackboard — only a hundred times as loud. Sparks were flying and everyone was screaming and by this time the truck had jackknifed and we were still moving forward."

Two seconds later, both vehicles veered to the right and plunged into space.

"I tried my best to keep my truck on the bridge," Steeves said later. "I never dreamed we would both end up in the river. There was no guardrail, and when I saw that my truck was headed for the edge, I thought, 'I have to get out, she's going to blow.' I jumped at the last minute, and I could feel her starting to go when I jumped. I don't remember hitting the ground. I jumped up and hollered at the men working there to run and get off the bridge."

Jumping from his moving truck, Steeves fell headlong into a series of steel reinforcing bars that were imbedded upright in cement. Despite the fact that his side was badly lacerated and one of the rods was driven into his leg, he got to his feet and scrambled to safety, blood spurting from his leg as he did so.

Then the first explosion came.

Bystanders watched in utter horror as the flying sparks set off by the collision ignited the gasoline that gushed from the ruptured tanker. The fuel seemed to burn evenly for a fraction of a second, then shredded the steel of the truck like the burst of a bomb. A waterfall of fire poured from the bridge as the compartmentalized fuel bays were torn open, one after the other. As each exploded, the sound ricocheted along the river, shook buildings a kilometre away, and sent a tower of flame higher than the trees. This was followed by a pall of smoke seen in Saint John.

In the dining room of the Mandarin House restaurant, which looks out on the Hammond River and the bridge over it, a waitress was taking meal orders at the time the crash occurred. Both she and the dining room patrons heard the colli-

sion, but none of them was prepared for the pillar of fire that roared up from the river below. "The waitress screamed and came running from the dining room," recalls Lily Yee, who with her husband owns the Mandarin House. "I grabbed the phone and called the fire department. Then I yelled at my husband and told him to get our papers and get out. I was afraid the whole place would burn. The customers left right away. They said they couldn't eat after what they had seen. We closed the place down for over an hour. Later on, Thelma Zwicker, one of the other waitresses here, told me she was glad she was off duty when the crash took place. She said that this was no place to be. It wasn't safe."

While all this was happening, Anna Lang's battered Buick hit the water, right side up.

"When we were being pushed along the bridge, there was so much racket," says Lang, "but when we went over the side my car seemed to spin around and I could see the restaurant. I knew it should have been behind me, though, and for a minute I had no idea where I was. I suppose the car was in the air at the time. Then I guess we went into the water. For a minute everything was silent and I can recall thinking, 'Oh God, it's all over.' Suddenly, there was water in the car."

A moment later the transport tractor fell into the river on its roof, a metre away. Then the shattered tanker landed on its side, disgorging burning gasoline into the water in shimmering, scorching, deadly waves. Further explosions came, each adding more fuel to the wild inferno. The

leaping, crackling, roaring flames obliterated all signs of life.

But there was life.

"My car sank right away," explains Lang, "and water started pouring in. I kept holding my breath until I thought my lungs would burst. The next thing I knew, Lana was holding Jaye and I was floating over them, out the right window. I remember hitting the surface and gasping for air, but the whole river was burning and I could still hardly breath. It was so *hot*.

"Because we had been to exercise class, both Lana and I had a lot more clothing on than we normally would have. I was wearing jeans and a couple of heavy sweaters over my tights and leotards. As soon as the jeans and sweaters got wet, they weighed a tonne so I knew I had to get rid of them if I was going to be any help to Lana and Jaye. By this time they had got to the surface, so I started swimming for shore.

"As I was swimming I was saying, 'Lana, I'll be back, I'll be back.' She never heard me say that and I never heard her say, 'Anna, please come back for me.' I guess we both thought these things but we never mouthed the words."

Now the fire was spreading farther and farther over the river. Rings of flame alternated with patches of clear water as Anna fought her way through the inferno towards shore, 40 metres away. "I tried to duck under each ring and then get my breath in the clear spaces," she says, "but that was not always possible. It was so hot on top, I felt better if I stayed under. Then I remember getting to shore and trying very hard to quickly take my outer clothes off. When I finally got rid of them, I went back in."

While Anna was struggling with her wet clothes, Lana Walsh and Jaye were having difficulties in the water.

"I was trying to hold Jaye up," she said later. "We had gone down several times and I was getting tired. So tired. And the heat was unbearable. Everything was burning. My big sweater was pulling me down and I was getting so tired that I was starting to give up. I wanted to save Jaye, but the heat was so bad. Everything was burning and I had to keep pushing his head under the water. Then I looked and he wasn't moving, and I thought he was dead. But then his eyelids moved. The water was burning and Jaye's hair was on fire. Then I saw Anna on the shore, but she seemed so far away.

"I saw blood pouring down her face. She was taking off her jeans and sneakers, and I can see her now splashing into the water. She came back for us. The water was burning but she really came back for us."

"As soon as I couldn't feel the bottom anymore, I started swimming," recalls Lang. "I decided to grab Jaye instead of his mother because I was afraid she might panic and drown us all. I knew if I got Jaye, she would hold on. That's what happened. He had taken swimming lessons the winter before and I think that's what saved him."

The young boy floated on his back and his mother held onto him with her left hand, keeping herself afloat with her right. When his hair began to burn, she pushed him under to put the flames out. "I finally got to them and grabbed Jaye by the shoulder and started pulling both of them after me. Every so often my hair would go on fire and I had to keep ducking to put it out. I believe Lana was in too much shock to do that.

"As we got closer to the shore, everything seemed to be so quiet. Jaye was very quiet and so was Lana. I guess there were people up on the bridge watching, although I was not aware of it. I was just too busy."

But not everyone was on the bridge watching.

Two local youths, Eric Sparks and Jack Chaisson, both 18, had been in a car behind the gasoline tanker. They had witnessed the accident, but had been able to stop before becoming involved in it.

When they saw the vehicles plunge off the bridge, they left their car and made their way down the south embankment to the edge of the river. Almost without thinking, Sparks took off his pants and waded into the water to help with the rescue. By this time Anna was approaching the shore with Jaye and Lana in tow.

"There was still a lot of burning gas around us, but I could see those guys ahead of me," recalls Anna. "They were standing on the bank and one had no pants on. I remember thinking, 'Why is he in his underwear?' Then I saw him coming into the water. I kept saying, 'Please help me God. I'm not going to make it.'

"Eric got to me just as my feet touched the

bottom again. He grabbed Jaye and handed him to Jack and then he got Lana. They had to carry them because Lana wasn't able to walk. At this point, I didn't want to look at her, or at Jaye. I didn't know what they looked like, if they were cut, had broken arms or anything. I didn't know what I had done to them."

Finally Anna managed to pull herself up onto the rocky shore, her head, face and neck now severely burned, her face bloody, and what was left of her clothes in tatters. She would not know until later that she had two cracked vertebrae in her back.

Even though they were now on shore, they were far from safe. Across the water the crackling flames engulfed more and more of the tanker, but still the flow of gasoline had not abated.

"We've got to get out of here right away," Jack said. "That thing is going to blow again."

He had no sooner said the words than the last of several explosions boomed across the water, spewing a geyser of steam, mud, flaming gasoline and hunks of shattered steel into the air. The earth shook and little Jaye clasped Jack Chaisson in a terrified but silent bear-hug. Eric knelt on the ground beside Lana, placed his arms under her back and legs and hoisted her into his arms. Anna, by now so exhausted she felt she would drop, wobbled unsteadily for a moment, then straggled along after the others, away from the flames. Steadily, painfully, doggedly, the group made its way along the rocky shore, crossed under the bridge and then, helped by several others including trucker Charles Steeves, managed to reach the top of the bank and safety.

The first ambulance arrived four minutes later.

*   *   *

Anna, Lana and Jaye were all hospitalized as a result of their ordeal. Anna's injuries were the most serious and she was incapacitated for the longest time. Her back healed on its own, but the third-degree burns to her face and head required skin grafting, plastic surgery and hair transplants. She was well enough, however, to fly to Ottawa two years later to receive her Cross of Valour — although she still claims she did not deserve it. She and Lana Walsh are still friends.

To this day neither feels safe crossing the Hammond River bridge.

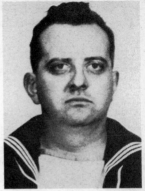

Partanen and Stringer

The sea was calm at first light, yet slate-grey and cold. Leaden clouds touched the horizon and the mist of morning wrapped the ship like a shroud. Across her clammy decks, rivulets of water drained into shallow pools and these reflected the dismal sky. Behind lay the coast of England, while ahead, an ocean away, was Canada and home. The ship had been away for weeks, and as always, the crew longed to return to Canada. Another few days and they would be there — or at least, most of them would be there.

The ship was called the *Kootenay*, a destroyer with 225 officers and crew on board. On this morning of October 23, 1969, she and eight other Canadian Navy ships were westbound out of the English Channel. They had been taking part in manoeuvres off the coast of Europe, but now that their work was done, they were heading for the open sea.

"We had just finished over six weeks of exercises and we were finally on our way home," recalls Mike Aris, a senior able seaman in the sonar branch. "All we wanted to do was stand our watches, relax a bit and go home. I had just been married in August of that year and this trip had begun in early September, so I was looking forward to its end. A lot of the guys felt the same way I did."

One of the ships with the *Kootenay* that morning was the *Saguenay*. Both had been ordered to break away from the rest of the formation in order to conduct full-power drills, high-speed runups in excess of 28 knots. The aircraft carrier *Bonaventure* and the rest of the task group were not involved in this particular endeavour. In fact, at the time the *Kootenay* began her drills, all of the other ships in the area were over the horizon.

Between 6:00 and 7:00 A.M., the *Kootenay* maintained an even 25 knots. Her speed was then gradually increased until 8:10, when the order "Full speed ahead, both engines" was given. This order was not customarily used during a full-power trial, but its use caused no confusion in the engine room. The ship was running well, and despite the dullness of the morning, the speed of the ship evoked a jauntiness of spirit that many of those who were there still remember.

At precisely 8:16, Lieutenant Al Kennedy, the engineer of the *Kootenay,* entered the engine room after having visited the boiler room. As he walked through, he spoke to the men and felt the two main engine gear boxes to see if they were hot. While both were quite warm, he had no trouble bearing the heat with the palm of his hand. He nodded at John MacKinnon and Eric Harman, who were at the throttles, and then stopped to talk with Chief Petty Officer Vaino (Ski) Partanen, who was there as well.

It was the last conversation Partanen would ever have.

Suddenly a sound, which would later be described by some as like the hiss of a welding torch and by others as like a crash, erupted in the engine room. The starboard gearcase exploded without warning, driving deadly shards of metal across the room. The high-speed pinion bearings within the gearcase itself had become overheated, and their heat combined with the oil vapour present in the air to cause a spontaneous explosion. Almost immediately the engine room was engulfed in flames and intense heat.

One of the men in the room, Able Seaman Mike Hardy, was thrown from an overhead catwalk, his clothes in flames. Lieutenant Kennedy bounded towards the port throttle in a vain attempt to close it. One and possibly two others in the room tried to do the same thing with the starboard throttle.

A white-hot sheet of flame flashed across the chamber, tore into seven crewmen who were close at hand and instantly snuffed out their lives before they knew what had happened. Three others were able to flee the inferno and one of these, Al Kennedy, somehow scrambled up the forward engine-room ladder and raced to the bridge to sound the alarm.

Several men who saw him during this time remember his soot-blackened face and clothes. And even though he was badly burned, with strips of flesh hanging from his face and arms, he was still coherent when he reached the bridge. He blurted out one of the first messages about the situation in the engine room, and then slumped to the deck, trembling in pain and shock. Someone gave him morphine from the captain's safe.

Even as he knew he was dying, Ski Partanen's thoughts were for the safety of the ship and the officers and men on it. He remained where he was in the engine room while the searing flames obliterated everything around him. He grabbed the phone to the wheelhouse and screamed, "Request permission to stop both engines." The request was relayed to the bridge, and the officer of the watch immediately ordered both engines stopped. By this time dense, acrid clouds of smoke were billowing through the ship.

"I was in the engine room a couple of seconds before the explosion," recalls Russell (Sandy) Saunders, an air force corporal on duty with the navy at the time. "I saw that there was no coffee there and I asked Mike Hardy to get some. However, because he was covered with grease, I decided to go for the coffee myself. That decision saved my life.

"I had just climbed the ladder from the engine

room and was in the act of stepping out into what we called Burma Road, a passageway down through the centre of the ship, when I noticed a terrific wind on my back. I was lifted from my feet and propelled forward. The next thing I knew I felt a tremendous crush as the right side of my body hit the mailbox by the cafeteria.

"Just as that was happening, somebody came out of the cafeteria and asked me what was wrong. I started to tell him, and as I did so, I looked back over my shoulder. Huge balls of fire were coming out of the afterhatch of the engine room. Momentarily a figure appeared in the flames, screaming, his clothes on fire and his hands and face burned raw.

"The fireballs seemed to be alive. They bounced from one side of the hall to the other and came right down Burma Road after me. I barged into the cafeteria to get away from the flames.

"There were several men there who were having a late breakfast because they had just come off watch. I remember that the petty officers were sitting at the table to my left, and that Sergeant Lou Stringer was in the first seat. Most of the men still had their heads down over their meals because the full impact of what had happened had not sunk in. Lou was the first to react.

"He asked me what was wrong, and before I even finished answering he was on his feet beside me. He had been around a little longer than the rest of us, and I suppose that was why he sensed the danger before the others. There were no escape hatches in the cafeteria."

By this time the fire had blocked the only other exit from the cafeteria and angry flames began inching their way across the ceiling. The appearance of the flames set off a wild stampede for the door that Saunders had just entered.

"Suddenly every man in the room seemed to be charging me," he recalls, "but I kept shouting that there was no escape that way, that Burma Road was full of fire. Stringer told the men to get down and get something over their faces to breathe through. Then he helped me keep people from going out into the hallway.

"Just opposite where we stood was the servery, with the opening to it covered by a corrugated metal door. We started pounding on that door and finally somebody opened it to see what the racket was. As soon as the opening appeared, people began piling through it, climbing up over the steam tables in order to get out through the galley. By this time, the whole place was starting to fill with smoke."

As the choking smoke poured into the cafeteria, the hysteria of the men trying to flee intensified. They screamed, cried, cursed, jostled one another, and climbed over each other in their wild and desperate rush to escape. Some flattened themselves on the deck, breathed through clothing and prayed for rescue. Others tried to push past Saunders and Stringer, towards what would have been certain death in the hallway outside.

"The pushing and shoving seemed to go on and on," says Saunders. "If Lou hadn't been beside me, a lot of guys would have died right there. The ones that were later rescued in the cafeteria owe their lives to him. And he was really responsible for getting the rest through into the galley where the cooks led them out.

"Until the day I die, I will never forget the screaming and the terrible things I saw that morning," continues Saunders with a shudder. "Men were crying, cursing and praying all at the same time. I heard somebody saying a rosary and I thought that wasn't such a bad idea, so I too cried out to God and asked Him to help me. I remember praying that I might see my wife and children again. At the time I had a son who was four years old and a daughter who had just been born, but I really thought they had seen their dad for the last time.

"The smoke became thicker and blacker, almost within seconds. It became harder and harder to breathe, and then, when you did breathe, the chemicals in the smoke and the heat from the fire seemed to burn right into your lungs. About that time I started to lose track of where I was or what I was doing.

"I remember losing and gaining consciousness while I was standing there. I couldn't see a thing in the black smoke, and after a while my throat didn't hurt anymore and I wasn't able to feel anything in my arms and legs. That was when I knew I was dying. I don't remember falling."

Elsewhere on the ship, John Montague was in his bunk at the time of the engine room explosion. He had been on watch from midnight until four that morning and had expected to sleep until about nine. His rest was interrupted.

"Just after 8:20, the telephone rang in my cabin," he recalls. "When I answered I heard Sub-Lieutenant Gerry Gadd shouting, 'Get out of there. The ship's on fire.' Almost at the same instant two persons burst into my cabin, coughing and gagging because of the thick, black, oily smoke. Because I was just wearing underwear shorts, I grabbed a pair of khaki trousers, but that was all the dressing I had time to do. One of the men who had come into my cabin was shouting out at someone, 'Open the hatch, open the hatch,' in reference to the main hatch which led to the upper deck.

"The hatch was open, but the black smoke made it look as if it was closed. The man then left my cabin and made a dash down the passageway to the ladder which led to the hatchway and to the exit to the upper deck.

From outside, there was little indication of the inferno raging below deck.

"I told the other guy we'd better get out as well. He was a wardroom steward who had been in the process of making up the officers' cabins when the explosion took place. Unfortunately he had joined the ship just prior to our leaving Halifax, and furthermore he was an air force private, which meant he hadn't been trained for this type of emergency and was not entirely familiar with the layout of the ship.

"Because of this, he hesitated to leave my cabin, so I grabbed him by his belt and literally pushed him all the way down the passageway to the ladder to the upper deck. Once we were out of the smoke he was okay. Later he thanked me."

When the fire on board started, the captain of the *Kootenay,* Commander Neil Norton, was in his cabin. Because he was some distance from the engine room, he noticed only a slight bump at the time of the explosion. He soon knew there was something seriously wrong, however, because within 15 seconds the entire ship seemed to be filled with smoke. Almost at the same time the announcement was made from the bridge: "All hands to emergency stations. Fire in the engine room. This is not a drill." With that, Norton and his executive officer raced to the bridge to take control. The ship's company were already on their way to emergency stations.

The officer of the watch at the time of the explosion was John Keenliside. He had given the order, "Full speed ahead, both engines," as well as the orders, "Stop both engines" and "All hands to emergency stations." Later he would tell a board of inquiry that by the time he had finished giving the emergency announcement the smoke had reached the bridge.

During this time, the inferno in the engine room was so terrible that any chance of men surviving there had long since vanished. The last man out, Able Seaman George (Dinger) Bell, had been going up an engine-room ladder at the time of the explosion and Leading Seaman Gary Hutton had pushed him to safety. Hutton did not survive. Even though Ski Partanen's last message was garbled, the man who took it understood from its tone that the situation was desperate. All hope had gone.

In the cafeteria, the crush of men trying to get out over the servery table went on, but at a slower and slower pace as the deadly smoke took its toll. Because it was over the burning engine room, the floor of the cafeteria was hot, so hot that some of the asphalt tiles were beginning to bubble in the area immediately above the gear cases where the fire had originally started. The cafeteria itself was a shambles: dishes, food and personal belongings littered the floor, and the taps on two large milk urns had broken open, spewing cold milk on the deck around Sandy Saunders, Lou Stringer and others. Even though several men collapsed in the cafeteria, the cooling effect of the milk prevented them from being burned alive.

"I could still hear the screams of other men," says Saunders today, "but I never heard Lou complain. He just kept on trying to get the men out of there. He was the least likely guy to stand with his back against the wall when the chips were down.

Ordinarily he was a spectator in sports and so on, but this time, when he was really needed, he stood by his men. When he was needed, he was brave in a way the others couldn't touch. I'll never forget him for that.

"After a time I somehow realized that we were lying on the floor, but I had lost all sense of direction and I could feel no pain. Then somehow through the smoke I could see light and the words 'where there's light, there's air' kept running through my mind. 'Where there's light, there's air. Where there's light, there's air.' I turned towards the light and kept breathing deeply in that direction. Then I heard someone ask a ridiculous question: 'Is there anybody alive down here?'

"A guy wearing a Chemox breathing apparatus was coming towards me, shining a light through the smoke. I tried to yell at him but because my throat was burned I couldn't make any sound. I did have some strength in my arms, though, and I was able to grab his leg as he went by. He half dragged, half carried me away. As we went, my arm touched something that was hot and I recoiled from it, although I welcomed the pain because it told me I really was alive. Finally we came to the hatchway and I remember seeing it through the smoke, clouded but yet bright. Then the moment I hit the fresh air, I passed out."

At about the same time as the fireballs were roaring down Burma Road, Mike Aris and another sailor were busy scrubbing Number 1 mess near the bow of the ship. At the instant of the explosion, both noticed that their ears popped, but there was no other indication that anything was wrong. Then a few seconds later the action alarm sounded.

"When the alarm sounds, it's normal procedure to get your life jacket and get out as quickly as possible," Aris explains. "If you don't, you're in trouble after the drill is over — and we just assumed that this was another drill. However, we soon changed our minds.

"The coxswain came up the ladder to the mess where we were and virtually screamed at us to get out of there. We knew from the tone of his voice that this was no exercise, so the speed with which we grabbed our gear and ran towards the emergency stations increased dramatically. Even today, my speed getting out never varies. I just go flat out and wait to see whether it's a drill or not, because the sound of the alarm always gives me a sick feeling.

"As we started out, we had no idea where the trouble was, but when we got to Burma Road we realized how serious things were. The whole passageway was full of black smoke, and it seemed to be getting thicker all the time. We proceeded as quickly as we could to what were called the wardroom flats. There was a ladder there and everyone was waiting his turn to go up. Most of the waiting was orderly, although one guy panicked and pushed some others out of the way and rushed up.

"While I was standing there waiting, I looked around and noticed the doors to sick bay swing open. Inside, the lights were extremely bright and the air seemed to be clear. It was so dark in the flats where we were standing that a few of the fellows grabbed quick breaths of fairly clean air before sick bay became just as engulfed with smoke as Burma Road.

"While the doors were open, I noticed a guy screaming and it took me a few seconds to realize that it was Dinger Bell. I didn't recognize him at first because his skin was black and burnt and it was hanging off his face and arms. At that point I remember being really scared."

As the fire continued to rage in the engine room, the nearby boiler room remained undamaged. Even though the men on duty there noticed a change in air pressure at the time of the explosion, they thought nothing of it. They did hear the emergency announcement, but doubted its seriousness. However, when smoke began to build up around them, they knew something was quite wrong. Yet by that time, even though they tried to telephone for direction, they were unable to do so. All communication channels with the other areas of the ship had failed. So, still without orders to the contrary, they continued their work.

Finally, however, fearing that they would be overcome if they remained where they were, they shut off the steam to the main engines, and following the advice of the petty officer in charge of the area, Clement Leo Bussiere, lay on the deck plates and breathed through damp clothing and rags. Fortunately, rescue was close at hand.

In all, more than 40 minutes had elapsed since the explosion, and during much of this period the *Kootenay* was technically out of control. The ship's

The engine room was gutted by the fire.

steering lines had burned out when the fire started, but because the boilers were still functioning, the vessel was able to continue on its way as if nothing had happened.

While all this was going on, officials on the bridge were desperately trying to assess the seriousness of the situation. But they were hampered in their efforts because of the smoke and the breakdown of communications, not only on the *Kootenay* itself, but elsewhere as well. For a time, all the radios on board failed to work, so none of the other vessels in the task group was aware that one of their number was in trouble. Even if one had been, the nearest was 27 kilometres away.

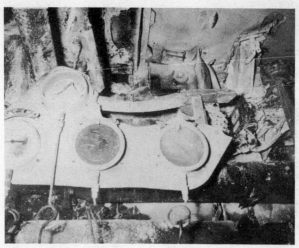

The remains of the port engine gauges.

During the time the bridge was attempting to call for help, most of the ship's company was pouring out onto the deck. Mike Aris remembers:

"We reached our emergency stations, and we were all pretty nervous. We pulled our life jackets around our necks and watched the smoke pour out of the ship. At this point no one knew whether we were going to abandon her or not. I noticed one guy who couldn't swim, so I offered him my life jacket, but he refused to take it. He kept saying he wouldn't need it, that we wouldn't be leaving. I'm afraid I wasn't that confident.

"As we stood there, we heard rumours that the fire was in the boiler room, right underneath where about 40 of us had collected. Somebody claimed there might be another explosion, so we all cleared out of there fast. We were then ordered to close the ventilation shafts to cut off the air from reaching below. Just as we started this, a stoker began screaming at us to leave the vents open because the smoke had to escape. The man was in bad shape. He had apparently been near the fire and knew that many of his friends were probably dead."

The deadly smoke from the engine room was still coursing through the *Kootenay* as the first rescue teams began assembling on the upper decks. Unfortunately, several of the vital Chemox breathing packs were so close to the fire area that they could not be reached. Those that were at hand were put to quick use. Several men donned diving masks and tanks in order to be able to function in the smoke. One man who did was Sub-Lieutenant Clarke Reiffenstein.

"We had to get to the valves to shut off the fuel feeding the starboard engine," he recalls. "These valves were located just ahead of the engine room, and I managed to crawl there using diving equipment. But when I got there I was unable to close the levers. Later the fuel was cut off from the boiler room. As I was coming back, I heard someone moaning and I crawled forward towards the engine room hatch. I found a dead body there, and not far from it, another guy who was still alive. I crawled with him to the wheelhouse.

"Then I crawled back, but I was afraid to stand up in all the smoke. I took off my mouthpiece and screamed, 'Anybody here need help?' I heard somebody in the galley and I went to him. He was in bad shape, all filled up with smoke, and he couldn't breathe the oxygen on my mouthpiece, so I had to drag him out."

The third time Reiffenstein returned below deck, two divers were with him. One was John Montague.

"I was one of eight divers on board at the time," says Montague, "and I remember Reiffenstein asking for help because he could hear voices coming from the boiler room. He couldn't get the afterdoor open which led to the boiler room because there was the body of a dead seaman leaning up against it."

After dislodging the body from in front of the door, Reiffenstein scrambled down the ladder into the boiler room. The five men he found there were badly shaken but alive.

"During all of this time the ship was still going ahead on the port screw," recalls Mike Aris. "There was no steering capability left, so we were going in a huge lazy circle at full speed. As we stood on the quarterdeck we saw red flares being fired from the bridge, and that certainly emphasized how serious the situation was. There were still no other ships in sight, so suddenly it was very lonesome.

"But radio contact was eventually made, and I still believe the most beautiful sight I have ever seen was the *Bonaventure* and all her escorts coming over the horizon at full steam, led by a half dozen or so of her helicopters. One by one they discharged foam, firefighters and breathing equipment. Then, as one of the helicopters took away the body of a man who had died, I felt like crying."

* * *

In all, nine men lost their lives and 53 others were injured in the explosion and fire on the *Kootenay* that cold October morning in 1969. And while those who were there all have different memories of the accident, none of them will ever forget it. Three years later, Crosses of Valour were awarded posthumously to Ski Partanen and Lou Stringer for their heroism that day. Partanen's body was found at his post in the engine room, while Sergeant Stringer died two days later from the after-effects of his ordeal.

Hynes

The Burin Peninsula is a narrow, sparsely populated, sometimes lonely strip of land jutting into the sea from the south coast of Newfoundland. One can drive for great distances and never see a fence, a farm, or in some areas, even a tree. In the summer, warm breezes caress this wild land and make it beautiful. In winter, biting gales sweep in from the ocean and the barren plains become as desolate as the surface of the moon.

Low hills, rocky outcrops and spongy swamps stretch to the horizon. Gnarled bushes, their tortured spines bent by the wind, cling to the soil in a desperate, never-ending struggle to survive. The coarse vegetation is soft underfoot, but difficult to walk on, like walking uphill on sand.

The main road on the peninsula is often deserted, even in summer. Yet this is not really surprising, because almost no one lives along it. Indeed, from the Trans Canada Highway in the north to the hamlet of Marystown, 150 kilometres to the south, there is but one village, a name beside a dot on the map.

But people do live on the peninsula, most of them in settlements bordering the sea. One of these is Jacques Fontaine, an attractive fishing village on Fortune Bay. Here, set amid weathered hills stretching back from the shore, are boat houses, clusters of well-kept homes, a modern high school, a post office and a cemetery. It was in that cemetery that I located the grave of the man whose story I had come to seek, the story of Thomas Hynes, the youngest recipient of the Cross of Valour.

Tom Hynes was only 19 when he died, but he died a hero, just as he told his schoolmates he would not long before graduating from Jacques Fontaine High School.

"Yes, that is what he said to them," recalls his mother today. "And even when they laughed at him, he stuck to his story. He told them just to wait, that his name would be in the papers, that he would die a hero. Well, I guess he was right."

The death of Tom Hynes is well remembered in Jacques Fontaine, but for that matter, so is his life. He lived here for virtually all of his 19 years, and he was as much a part of the village as the parish church is.

"He went away for about six months," his

mother explains. "That was to Manitoba to work for the CPR. But when the railway laid him off in the fall, he came back home. I don't think he really knew what he wanted to do. In the grade 11 yearbook at school he said that his plans for the future were unknown. Maybe he knew he didn't have a future. He often said he would never marry. He didn't have a girlfriend."

Tom Hynes was a popular young man in the village. With his rather shy manner, his shock of thick brown hair and his ready smile, he was welcome in every home. He played hockey, loved it and was good at it, but he also enjoyed driving his old snowmobile, one of the few things he ever owned. He never had much money, nor for that matter, did anyone in his family.

"My late husband was a fisherman," says Mrs. Hynes, "and because there were 14 in the family, we always had to struggle to make ends meet. We had four daughters and 10 sons, and Tom was our sixth child. He was such a happy boy, always kidding and joking and making other people laugh. That was why everybody was so shocked when he died. I missed him a lot when he went away to work on the railroad, and I was happy to see him come home. But now he's gone forever. I think of him every day, and of course I will never forget the day he died."

The day Martha Hynes remembers so vividly was December 29, 1977. It was the day her son Tom left the house for the last time. "He had just received his first unemployment cheque after being laid off by the railway," she continues. "That morning he had gone out to the post office and had taken his cheque and his hockey equipment with him. I assumed he was going somewhere to play hockey. But then he came back, left his hockey stuff here and went out again. I didn't know where he was going."

At about the same time as Tom was returning home with his hockey equipment, a group of young boys in the neighbourhood were playing along the shore of a partially frozen pond, beside the main highway a short distance away. Because the day was sunny and cold, and they were on their Christmas holidays, they decided to test the ice. A day or so earlier it had not been hard enough to support them, but today might be different.

As they gingerly eased out onto the surface of the pond, air bubbles ran every which way under the ice, and it began to crack, so everyone knew it was still not hard enough for hockey. With that, two of the group, Wade Hynes, Tom's 12-year-old brother, and his cousin Keith Hynes, who was four years younger, started to search along the shoreline for pucks that had been lost during hockey games the previous winter.

The two plodded through the underbrush, talking and laughing as they went. Once or twice they stopped and tossed bits of wood out onto the pond and watched as they skittered across the frozen surface. Then they noticed Tom standing on the far shore. On the spur of the moment, and with very little thought to the danger, the two youngsters decided to cross the ice to see him. The fact that he was older and popular with everyone made them want to be with him.

Wade went first, walking slowly a step or two in front of Keith. The younger boy was slightly to one side. Tom watched from the far bank. The ice held.

The two boys went farther and farther, gliding their heavy winter overshoes along the slick surface. Under their feet, the ice looked like glass, with thousands of ice bubbles streaming in every direction. Through the ice near the shore, they could see large rocks on the bottom, and long silky patches of weeds growing almost to the surface. But as they moved closer to the centre of the pond, the water became deeper and the bottom disappeared, and both boys felt afraid.

With a loud cracking sound, like a tree breaking in a storm, the ice started to give way.

Wade sensed the danger first and shouted a warning to Keith before spinning around and racing for the nearest land. When he reached it, the other boys who were watching cheered because none of them had ever seen him move so fast.

But the cheers did not last.

Out on the pond, Keith seemed to hesitate for a second, but for some reason decided he could reach the opposite side. He moved cautiously at first, as if confused, but then dashed towards a point of land 30 metres away.

He did not get there. The echoes of ice cracking swept the surface of the pond, and before he had gone half a dozen steps, Keith lost his footing and plunged into the frigid water.

"I was really scared," he admits today. "I began to scream, because I didn't know how deep it was. I was also very cold. I remember holding onto the ice and trying to get myself up on it, but I kept slipping off. My clothes were heavy in the water and I couldn't get a grip on anything. I guess everybody was watching me, but I didn't think of that at the time."

Tom Hynes had been watching, and almost before Keith knew what had happened, his older cousin was out onto the ice trying to help.

"He came towards me, but the ice broke under him too," Keith remembers. "I knew he would still try to come for me and he did."

As Keith floundered in the deep water, Tom eased closer and closer to him, half swimming and half supporting himself by grabbing at the edge of a large sheet of floating ice. He told Keith that he would be all right, and urged him to stay close to the ice sheet.

The younger boy did as he was told, but continued to scream in terror as the cold water soaked through his clothes, poured into his overshoes and pulled him down.

"Then Tom got under me and started pushing me up," says Keith. "But I couldn't get a grip on anything and I kept slipping. I know if he had not been there I would have died. I was cold and scared."

While the grim struggle went on in the centre of the pond, Wade and his friends looked on in desperation, wanting to help but not really knowing what to do. Once or twice one of them started out on the ice, but each time it cracked so much they retreated. Finally, somebody found a long wooden stake half-hidden by dead grass and scrubby pine boughs. The boys pulled the length of wood free and carried it to the shore.

Then the oldest of the group, 14-year-old Leo Farrell, slid the stake onto the ice and slowly crawled out towards Keith and Tom, while another youngster ran for help.

In the meantime, Keith and Tom continued to flounder near the centre of the pond. With tears streaming down his face, his features constricted by fear, and his voice hoarse from screaming, Keith fought to hold on. He had slipped down several times, but each time Tom dived below the surface, grabbed him and pushed him back to the ice edge. Finally Tom managed to push Keith half out of the water so that the upper part of the younger boy's body rested on the ice.

"I can't remember whether Tom was still saying anything to me or not," says Keith. "All I know is that when he pushed me up, I didn't know he was in trouble himself."

But Tom was indeed in trouble. He still laboured almost mechanically, yet with each second that passed he grew more and more exhausted. The effort needed to hoist Keith onto the ice was great, and the numbing effect of the terrible cold was now unbearable. He dived one last time and pushed Keith as high as possible. Then, too tired to struggle anymore, he lost his grip and slipped beneath the ice.

Although the onlookers did not realize it, Tom Hynes was dying.

About 100 metres away, Keith's mother was working in the kitchen when she heard screams at the door. "I don't remember which of the kids was there," Zita Hynes says today. "I just know that when I heard the word 'ice' I panicked. I never even thought of a coat. I just headed for the pond."

It took Zita less than a minute to run from her house to the little path that leads down to the pond — but she was already too late to save Tom.

"When I got there, I saw Leo kneeling on the ice, with Keith holding on to the end of a wooden stake. I never saw poor old Tom. I didn't even know he was there. I saw Keith's cap out there, but I never saw Tom at all.

"Leo stayed where he was, and Keith held on

until somebody came with a rope and they were able to pull him out. But then, as soon as they got Keith to the shore, Wade and the others were yelling about Tom being gone. I really didn't know what they meant because I saw nothing of him. At the time I was just so grateful that Keith was safe."

Even though he was almost totally numb with the cold, Keith was still able to grab the rope when it was thrown to him. He held on and was swiftly pulled over the ice to shore. Two minutes later he was getting warm in his own home.

Not long after Keith was pulled from the pond, the telephone rang at the Royal Canadian Mounted Police detachment in Burin, 75 kilometres to the south. Constable Fabian Sutton took the call. "I had only been at the detachment for three weeks or so, and I was still not too familiar with the area," recalls Sutton. "So Sergeant Conrad went with me to the scene of the accident. It's a fairly long drive, and by the time we got there, neighbours had recovered the body and the local parish priest had notified the next of kin."

Martha Hynes recalls how she was told of her son's death: "I heard somebody at the door, and when I opened it, Father Kevin Bennet was standing there. Before he even opened his mouth, I said 'Tom's dead, isn't he?' I don't know how I knew, I just knew."

The priest stood there for a second and then quietly nodded his head.

Tom Hynes had died a hero.

Jean Swedberg

"So you are driving to Merritt," said the young woman at the counter. "You will love the town. I used to spend my holidays there, but I never seem to get back much anymore. I wish I was going with you."

With that, she handed me the keys to the car I had just rented and told me to enjoy my trip. I thanked her, glanced at the map and eased the little sedan into the Vancouver traffic. My journey, I reasoned, would take about four hours.

That estimate was wrong.

Perhaps it is *possible* to drive from Vancouver to Merritt in four hours; I just know it was not possible for me. For one thing, Merritt, an interior town, can be reached from the west only by two relatively circuitous routes. And because both of these lead through some of Canada's most spectacular scenery, no one but the most jaded traveller can avoid slowing down from time to time. Even after one has seen the glories of the Fraser River and such postcard places as Hope, Hell's Gate and Manning Park, the last few kilometres into Merritt are still surprising.

For one thing, the town of 8750 is nestled in a valley and surrounded on all sides by rolling, pine-studded hills that seem to go on forever. The valley is called the Nicola, after an Indian chief of long ago. Merritt was originally called The Forks, but when coal mining and ranching brought the railway in 1906, the settlement was renamed Merritt to honour one of the rail promoters.

Today, three primary industries support the community: lumbering, with three major sawmills and several smaller ones producing a variety of products; mining, with three copper mines and extensive coal exploration; and ranching, with some of the world's largest cattle spreads ranging across the area's "Empire of Grass." Indeed, to a visitor, the rolling rangeland looks like the setting for all those cowboy movies that used to play in theatres on Saturday afternoons.

To the south of the town, high on a hill overlooking the valley, is a viewing place from which it is possible to see the entire town spread out below. I stopped at the spot and tried to picture what it must have been like to stand there in earlier times, before there was a town; then later on as settlers arrived. I also imagined what it must have been like on the night of Wednesday, September 4, 1974.

That was the night the Valnicola Hotel burned to the ground.

The blaze could be seen from the promontory, of course, as indeed it could be seen from almost anywhere in the valley. Because the fire was in the early evening, at the end of a long, beautiful day, many people were out of doors, and a crowd of 2000 gathered to watch as the hotel was razed.

Among them was a young man named Dean Swedberg, who had a deeply personal reason for being there. As he stood on the pavement staring into the flickering flames, his heart ached in a way only those who have suffered a similar experience can know. Dean Swedberg knew that his dear mother was dying in the inferno in front of him.

"I lived only a short distance from the hotel," he recalls, "and every night I would phone there and talk to my mother. That night when I called no one answered, even though I let the phone ring and ring. That was when I decided to go over to the hotel and see what was wrong. But long before I got there, I expected the worst.

"I stood on the street and asked everybody I knew if they had seen my mother. I guess no one had, but they didn't want to come right out and tell me. Different ones would say, 'Oh yes, I think I saw her at such and such a place.' Then someone else would say they thought she was somewhere else.

"It was a hard thing waiting there so long, but by the middle of the night I knew. I waited until morning, until her body was found. Then I went home. By that time it was all over. My mother was gone."

*   *   *

Jean Parker Cunningham was born in Tarbalton, Scotland, on July 21, 1924. As the third youngest in a family of 11, she was raised to believe that independence was a virtue, that being a burden to others was unacceptable. It was not surprising, then, that as soon as she was old enough to do so, she enlisted in the air force. Because the Second World War was underway at the time, scores of strangers in uniform were everywhere. One of them was a handsome, fair-haired young man who wore the blue serge of the Royal Canadian Air Force. His name was Stan Swedberg.

In due course, the quiet, studious, rather reserved young Canadian met the sprightly Scottish lass whose job involved military communications. For a time the two were little more than acquaintances, but gradually they were more and more often in each other's company. Finally, and to the surprise of no one who knew them, Stan and Jean decided to get married. The wedding took place in Scotland in 1945. One year later the newlyweds came to Canada.

The young couple settled in Manitoba, and it was while there that Stan Swedberg had an accident that almost killed him.

"When I was nine or 10, Dad was almost burned to death," explains Dean. "He was a pipefitter-welder at a smelter in Flin Flon. One day he was working inside a large tank and the thing exploded. The door to the outside was locked for some reason, and by the time they got him out, he had third-degree burns over much of his body. He suffered terribly as a result, and had to spend more than six months in a hospital in Winnipeg. Because of his accident, he understood what it was like to be burned; what it was like to die in a fire . . . "

Some years later, Stan and Jean and their family of five daughters and two sons moved to British Columbia, where Stan obtained employment on construction projects in and around the community of Merritt. As time passed and the family grew older, Jean began to feel as though she needed to get out of the house.

She had always been active in civic organizations, particularly in the Eastern Star, and she loved to play bingo — sometimes as often as three and four times in a week. Because she had never driven a car, she looked for a part-time job that was within walking distance of her home. The job she found at the 32-room Valnicola Hotel was the last job she would ever have. She held it for almost five years.

The Valnicola was not an old hotel; it had been built only 13 years earlier. But its ownership had changed several times. In September 1974, Mr. and Mrs. Gordon Sykes and Mr. and Mrs. Jack Egan were the proprietors.

The building was a two-storey frame structure, with a coffee shop, dining room, lobby and lounge running across the front, facing onto Voght Street, the main thoroughfare to the east. At the back, 10 bedrooms ran the length of the ground floor, while 20 more were located on the second storey. Much of the interior of the hotel was constructed of knotty pine, varnished to a shiny lustre.

The fire completely destroyed the old Valincola Hotel, shown above.

"It was a combination of the wood and the varnish that caused the building to burn so rapidly," says Jack Egan today. "I was in Vancouver the night the hotel was destroyed, but the firemen told me how quickly it went up. By the time I was called and I drove back here, it was all over."

On the evening of the fire, Jean Swedberg arrived at the hotel and began her duties as night clerk, looking after the front desk, answering the telephone and responding to requests from overnight guests.

One of those guests was a young man who occupied room 9 on the ground floor at the rear of the hotel. Whether Mrs. Swedberg ever saw him is not known. It is known, however, that the occupant of this room had a pizza delivered at approximately 8:00 P.M. It was later determined that he had lit a fire under the bed, then escaped the conflagration by going out a window at the rear. Still later, it was learned that the young man had come to Merritt to try out for a local hockey team, and because he was cut from the team, decided to vent his frustration by setting the hotel on fire. A day or so after the fire, Royal Canadian Mounted Police and officials from the fire marshall's office were able to trace the youth through the pizza delivery. He was arrested.

The fire was first noticed by Jacqui Gerow, another employee at the Valnicola. Initially the blaze seemed insignificant, and Ms. Gerow and one or two others who came to her assistance felt they could extinguish the flames themselves. They tried to do so, but within seconds the fire flared up, the bedclothes and curtains ignited and suddenly the room was in flames.

Gerow ran to call the fire department while Jean Swedberg and others went to the restaurant and lounge to tell the patrons in those rooms to flee. At first no one hurried to move, apparently because they could neither see any fire nor smell any smoke, and because there did not appear to be any immediate danger.

But Mrs. Swedberg knew differently. Leaving others to convince the lounge customers to leave, she rushed into the ground floor residential area of the hotel and raced from room to room, pounding on doors and shepherding occupants from the building.

As she did so, the crackling of flames could be heard in the hallway behind her. Room 9 was gutted in seconds. Billowing smoke poured from it. Already the doorjambs and walls outside the room were ablaze. Guests who came to their doors had only to glance past Jean to understand the need for urgency. One or two attempted to grab belongings, but most dropped everything and raced for the nearest exit.

The flames spread rapidly in the hallway, consuming everything as they moved. Within seconds, dense, grey-black smoke made it impossible to see more than a few paces, yet Mrs. Swedberg continued, her eyes stinging and her lungs screaming for air.

Finally, the last guest on the ground floor was safe.

By this time, all of the coffee shop and lounge

patrons were outside as well and the first fire siren was shrieking into the night. Volunteer firefighters left whatever they were doing and hastened to help, while RCMP officers, both on duty and off, converged on the Valnicola. As the crowds gathered, an instant traffic jam built up in front of the hotel.

In the meantime, Dean Swedberg's phone calls to his mother went unanswered.

People who were there that night remember seeing her rush from the ground floor hallway, past the ringing telephone, to the fresh air near the front doors. Then, after catching her breath and rubbing her stinging eyes, she turned back and went up the stairs that led from the lobby to the second floor bedrooms. She knew there were several occupants in those rooms, because she had seen most of them when they checked in earlier in the day. Now, as she fought her way up the stairs, a few terrified guests were coming down.

When Mrs. Swedberg finally reached the top of the stairs, she turned to the right and groped her way from room to room, pounding on each door and shouting for everyone to leave. Already the hallway smoke was starting to seep into many of the rooms, so guests who had been undecided about what to do had their minds made up for them.

The roaring inferno that was devastating the ground floor of the hotel had yet to reach the floor above, but the billowing smoke obliterated everything, including the hallway lights, which were still functioning. By this time, only Jean Swedberg's familiarity with the hotel floor plan assisted her. After five years at the Valnicola, she not only knew how many rooms there were on either side of the stairway, but she also knew the precise location of the rooms, and exactly who was in each.

To some extent, it was this familiarity that killed her.

No sooner had she succeeded in getting everyone out of the rooms on one end of the floor than she turned and moved as quickly as possible in the opposite direction. One or two guests who encountered her were already on their way out, but she feared a male occupant of the last room on her right might be trapped. Now, almost by instinct, she felt her way towards his room. As she did so, she coughed repeatedly and tried to ignore the pain in her eyes and throat. By now the smoke was black.

Out on Voght Street the first fire truck was in place, and harried firefighters were connecting hoses to the nearest hydrant. Dense clouds of smoke and sickly red-orange flames poured from the central portion of the building, as the bright neon sign in front of the hotel gleamed ghoulishly in the night. On all sides gawking crowds watched the inferno and hampered the efforts of the police, who were attempting to move the sightseers out of danger.

Gordon Sykes, one of the hotel owners, was on the scene almost from the beginning, and he later told reporters that his building was consumed so quickly almost nothing was saved from it. He tried to get into room 9 to make sure no one was trapped there, but was driven back by the flames. Some of

51

the first police officers and firefighters also attempted to check for missing patrons, but they too were forced out.

In the meantime, Jean Swedberg was frantically making her way through the blackness towards the last room. Behind her, flames were roaring up the staircase, and there was no hope of turning back. Nevertheless, she stumbled along, fighting to get her breath. Then, just as she reached the room she was seeking, she choked on the terrible smoke and fell to the hallway floor. Late the next morning her body was found in the charred rubble, directly below where that last room had been.

What she did not know was that the occupant of the room she was so desperately fighting to reach had sensed the danger and escaped through an upper window.

Later it was determined that a man named Harry Navokshanoff, who had a room on the second floor of the hotel, also perished in the fire. There is reason to believe he may have been outside during the time Jean Swedberg was searching for guests on the upper floor. Some believe that he returned to his room to retrieve personal items and was trapped while doing so.

Today, Jack Egan credits Mrs. Swedberg with the rescue of at least 12 people. He regards her as a true hero, a woman with depths of courage no one had imagined. "She was truly a delightful person," he recalls. "She had such a bubbling personality that it was almost impossible to be depressed when she was around.

"Jean enjoyed her work and loved meeting people. She was also totally reliable," he says. "She was working at the hotel when I bought the place, so I didn't hire her. I kept her on, however, because she was so good at her job."

With that, I concluded my visit to Merritt and packed my bags for the return drive to Vancouver. As I checked out of the new Valnicola Hotel, I sensed the spirit of Mrs. Jean Swedberg. She died a hero, and I was touched by her memory.

Mary Dohey

The big Air Canada jet lumbered out to the runway, received clearance for takeoff, and roared into the sky at precisely 4:15 P.M. Below and behind, Calgary looked like a toy town on the edge of the prairie. Tiny trucks raced along tiny roads, and the dots that had been cars disappeared. For a time the mountains were visible, but soon even they were gone.

Within minutes, Flight 812, bound for Toronto and Montreal, reached its cruising altitude. Far below, the checkerboard prairie was another world, familiar yet remote, for on this plane, as on every aircraft that has ever flown, reality is largely confined to the activities within the plane itself. And that night, on board that airliner, reality would become a horror beyond words.

It all came about because of one man.

Paul Joseph Cini was the 27-year-old son of a Maltese ship engineer. He grew up in Glasgow, Scotland, but when he was 17, he emigrated to Canada. He settled in Calgary and held a number of jobs there, one of which was rodman for the city survey department. After a while, however, he became disenchanted with surveying and decided to move to the United States. That was in 1964.

For the next seven years, his life was a litany of failures, both personal and professional. He became, among other things, a soldier, a car thief, a truck driver and a father. When he boarded Air Canada's Flight 812 on November 12, 1971, he was employed as a record salesman. He had lost his only child when the infant's mother put him up for adoption soon after he was born. He saw the baby once.

During the summer and early autumn of 1971, the inadequacies of his life had been bothering Cini. His opinion of himself had never been high, but now it was even lower than usual. He felt he had to do something, anything, in order to prove to himself and to the whole world that he was important. That was why he decided to hijack a plane.

In order to prepare for his mad escapade, Paul Cini started acquiring the paraphernalia he would need. In due course, he purchased a black balaclava, a wig, some dynamite, a shotgun and a parachute. With these, he reasoned, he could take over a plane, collect a ransom, and then parachute from the aircraft and disappear without a trace. As he went about securing the items he wanted, he drank, often to excess.

Finally he was ready. But he had not counted on meeting someone like Mary Dohey.

Dohey was a stewardess on the plane Cini picked to hijack. And, while his life had been in turmoil as an adult, hers had been chaotic as a child. But Mary Dohey had overcome her upbringing and made a success of herself, while Paul Cini had traded his past for a present that was anything but praiseworthy.

Mary Dohey was the youngest in a family of 14. She was orphaned when she was only three, and in the years thereafter was passed around to several foster homes. She was abused in some, lonely in most, but unbelievably resilient in them all. She put herself through school, and for a time became a teacher in Newfoundland. When she realized that a career in teaching was not what she wanted, she went back to her studies and obtained her Registered Nurse's certificate, specializing in psychiatry.

At one time, a woman wishing to be an airline stewardess had to be a nurse. It became almost natural, then, that Mary Dohey began looking for a career in the air. She longed to travel, and the idea of getting paid to do so was appealing. Air Canada, or Trans-Canada Airlines, as the company was formerly known, was looking for stewardesses. Dohey was accepted.

"I have enjoyed this life," she says today, "but of all the flying I've done, the night of the hijacking was something I will never forget. If I live to be a million, I will never get over that nightmare."

For Dohey and the others on Air Canada Flight 812, the nightmare began less than an hour out of Calgary. A short, curly-haired, swarthy man sitting in seat 2B in the first-class section bolted down a vodka and orange and then left his seat to go to a washroom at the front of the plane. He wore a long, oversized beige trenchcoat and carried a shopping bag.

Five minutes later, John Arpin, the 48-year-old purser on the flight, heard a noise behind him. He turned and looked straight into the muzzle of a sawed-off, double-barrelled shotgun. A grotesque-looking figure in a trenchcoat, black balaclava and black wig was sitting at a small table in the otherwise empty first-class lounge. The person holding the gun threatened to blow Arpin's head off unless he did what he was told.

"Sit over here," roared a male voice from under the black hood.

Arpin sat down.

"Take this and show it to the captain, and tell him to follow these instructions to a T," ordered the man.

He handed Arpin a sheet of yellow paper. The purser started to read.

"That's for the captain, not you," shrieked the man, and he jammed the gun into Arpin's face.

At that point, Mary Dohey walked into the lounge. She was about to speak to Arpin when she saw the gun.

"Sit down," demanded the figure in the black hood.

"Sit down, Mary," said Arpin. "It's for real."

As Mary took a seat beside the purser, the man in the mask swung the shotgun over to her and placed both barrels up against her forehead.

"Now, take that note to the captain," he said to Arpin, "and be quick about it. If you are not back right away, I'm killing your stewardess. Now you," he said, referring to Mary, "get over there by that window. Stand with your back against it and stare straight ahead. If you move, I'll blow your head off."

Mary went over to the window and Arpin disappeared into the cockpit. There he handed Captain Vern Ehman, a 43-year-old pilot from Montreal, the sheet of yellow paper. On it was a 506-word message that began with "Welcome aboard the original doomsday flight" and ended with "There'll be no heroes tonight, for tonight we all will die." The note demanded a ransom of $1.5 million and instructed the captain to fly to Great Falls, Montana. The money was to be collected there, and according to the note, had to be delivered to the plane by a woman.

While Arpin was on the flight deck delivering the note, the hijacker produced a 60-stick dynamite bomb. He handed Mary two wires protruding from it and told her to hold them apart. "If you don't," he snarled, "these wires will complete a circuit and this bomb will explode. If you want to die right now, you can let them touch." With that, he ordered her to sit beside him, with her back against the side of the plane. "Stare straight ahead," he repeated.

"I did exactly as he told me," Mary Dohey

Mary had to tell and retell her story.

recalls. "I had one wire beside my little finger and another by my thumb, and I held them that way for over four hours. But my God, I was terrified, so terrified. I had to keep staring ahead, so I looked across to a window at the other side. I knew the awful situation we were in, and I thought I would likely be dead before Johnny Arpin got back from the cockpit. All this time I was praying, praying harder than I'd ever prayed before."

As the seconds ticked away and Arpin had still not returned, the man with the shotgun became more and more agitated.

"I could see his eyes through the slits in the black hood," Dohey says with a shiver, "and I could tell he was pretty jumpy. Then I noticed that his trigger finger was trembling.

"When I saw that, I was sure I was dead, so I

made my peace with God. I was prepared to die. Then suddenly the gun started waving around and it went off."

Today Mary grimaces as she recalls the incident.

"The barrel was right beside my ear when the shot was fired," she says. "My head was ringing from the sound as the shot went into a wall."

The blast thudded into the cockpit bulkhead and tore a fist-sized hole through it. Spent pellets, dust and debris showered down on the second officer, and John Arpin was sure Mary was dead. He hurried back to the lounge.

As he did, he heard the hijacker say to Mary, "I'm sorry, I didn't mean to do that." She took up the cue.

"I know you didn't, dear. You don't want to hurt us, do you?" Her soft voice and sympathetic manner confused Paul Cini, the man in the disguise. She began to talk to him, hoping to gain his confidence. "My name is Mary," she said.

"Is that really your name?" Cini asked.

"Yes, it is," she answered. "Do you like it?"

"Yes, it's a nice name."

"Well, then, you may call me Mary. What is your name?"

"It's Dennis," lied Cini.

"Okay, Dennis," said the stewardess, "may I hold your hand?" With that, she took the hijacker's hand in hers, all the while talking to him in a gentle, caring tone.

"I talked to him as I have never talked to anyone before or since," she recalls. "I asked him about himself and I told him about me. We covered almost every topic I could think of, from the weather to sports, to jobs, to children. When I told him I was one of 14 children, he laughed and told me that was a lot of kids. I knew then that he liked children, and I told myself that fact might be something I could use later on. I was trying to find anything I could to calm the guy. The talking was so hard, though. The saliva in my mouth kept drying up, I was so scared."

When Arpin returned from the flight deck, Cini demanded to know if the captain understood the message.

"Yes," answered Arpin. "We're to go to Montana, pick up the money, then go to Regina, release the passengers, load the aircraft full of guns and ammunition, and head for Ireland."

"That's right," Cini agreed.

"But where does the money come from?" Arpin asked.

"Air Canada supplies the money," Cini yelled. "Go and tell the captain that."

Arpin returned to the cockpit with the message. He also told Ehman that the hijacker's name was Dennis and that the stewardess was sitting beside him holding his hand, trying to calm him down.

"Good," replied the pilot. "Keep me posted." With that he radioed Winnipeg ground control and passed on the new instructions. A few minutes earlier, at 5:15, it had been Winnipeg that gave Ehman the heading for Great Falls. Already the plane had been in the air for more than an hour.

During the flight into the United States, Cini would flare up at a moment's notice. Just when Mary began to feel that things might get better, they got worse. The hijacker complained of the heat in the plane, so the temperature was lowered. Arpin asked if he could put his coat on, but when he did, Cini saw the gold braid around the cuffs of the jacket and accused Arpin of being with the Federal Bureau of Investigation. When Arpin was asked about his nationality and said he was French, Cini shrieked, "It's good that you're not English, because I'm going to kill every Englishman on this plane."

Because the shotgun blast was loud enough to be heard by the passengers, Arpin asked Cini how the noise should be explained to them.

"Tell them a light bulb blew," the hijacker snapped. "Tell them whatever you want."

Arpin walked back to the first-class section and informed the passengers of the hijacking. "And if our guest comes back here," he warned, "don't let on that any of you are English. He told us he would kill anyone who was English."

Most of the passengers remained calm, although two got up and ran down the aisle towards the back of the plane. A few asked for drinks.

Shortly after Arpin returned to the lounge, assistant purser Philip Bonné entered. Up to that point, he did not know of the hijacking, nor did most of the passengers in the rear economy section of the plane. Cini ordered Bonné to sit down beside Arpin.

"What nationality are you?" Cini asked him.

"I'm French Canadian."

"Well then, I'll blow your head off. The FLQ would be proud of me and DeGaulle would turn over in his grave."

No one knew what this meant.

A few seconds later, Cini reached into the pocket of his trenchcoat and pulled out two bundles of dynamite. There were five sticks in each bundle.

"Now, I'm going to light these fuses and blow up the plane," he said.

Mary Dohey turned to him. "But Dennis, why would you do that, dear? You're going to hurt a lot of people. Do you know those people?"

Cini changed his mind. Instead, he took one stick of dynamite and pushed it into John Arpin's mouth. He then aimed the shotgun at Arpin's head.

Again Mary interceded. "Dennis, dear," she whispered, "why don't you put the safety catch on the gun?"

Cini became confused.

"Sit over there," he roared at Bonné. The assistant purser moved to the seat across the table from Mary. "Now take her hands," Cini demanded.

Bonné did so.

"Hold her hands so tight I can see the whites of your knuckles," Cini snapped.

While this was happening, John Arpin slowly withdrew the dynamite from his mouth. Cini saw him and jammed the explosive back in again. Then he apparently changed his mind, grabbed the dynamite and ordered Mary Dohey to smell it.

"My darling, I don't know anything about dynamite," she protested.

Cini set the stick on the table.

By this time, the plane had reached Great Falls, but Cini ordered it to circle the airport until the money he had demanded was ready. As soon as Captain Ehman received a radio message that the money was at the airport, he landed the DC-8. A police secretary walked out to the plane and tied the suitcase she carried onto a leather strap Bonné lowered from the aircraft. Bonné hauled the case containing the money into the plane and Ehman took off again. Fifteen minutes had passed.

As soon as the jet was at its cruising altitude, Cini ordered Arpin to count the money. As he did so, he realized, to his horror, that the suitcase contained only $50 000, not the $1 500 000 Cini wanted. Fortunately the hijacker did not notice the discrepancy.

"By this time, I realized just how mad the whole escapade was," recalls Mary. "It was a terrible, terrible nightmare, and I really expected we were all going to die. I made a pact with God at that time," she continues. "I told Him I would gladly die, but He had to show me a way to save the passengers. Then I recalled that the hijacker had seemed pleased when I told him I came from a family of 14, that he seemed to like kids."

Mary turned to Cini. "Dennis, I hear the children crying," she said.

"Do you mean there are kids on here?" Cini asked, apparently dumbfounded that that could be so.

"Oh yes," she said, "and I can hear them

crying. The dear little things are so tired and hungry. They don't know what's happening."

Cini reacted in fury.

"Go up and tell that captain," he said to Arpin, "to go back to Great Falls and let the people off. I am going to need the space for the ammunition."

Ehman swung the plane around and returned to Great Falls. The 118 passengers began leaving.

"Now," Cini barked at Arpin, "I have a blue suitcase on this plane. I want you to get it — *now!* I'll give you 10 minutes, and if you are not back with it then, I am going to kill this stewardess." He handed Arpin a baggage tag and checked his watch. Arpin scrambled down the ramp.

As soon as the purser had gone, Cini ordered Mary to turn around. Then he placed the muzzle of the shotgun against the back of her neck. She knew he was watching the time.

"Those minutes were some of the worst of my entire life," she says. "I could feel the cold steel on my neck and I really thought I would be killed — particularly when Johnny was delayed."

"Well, your time is up," Cini told her. Then he cocked the hammer of the gun. Mary asked if she could turn around. Cini consented.

"When I turned, he put the gun up against my forehead. But that was better than behind me, because I didn't think he could face me and kill me. I started pleading for him to give Johnny a bit more time. I told him how hard it would be to find one suitcase among all the others."

Just as Arpin returned, and after the last passenger was off, Cini leaned close to Mary and whispered, "Do you want to leave? If you want to leave, you can go."

Dohey was momentarily stunned by the sudden turn of events, but then she realized that if she left, the hijacker would blow up the plane. "I was worried about the pilot and the rest of the crew," she says. "I knew I had to fight to save them. By this time, I had developed some rapport with the hijacker and I knew that if I could not control him, we would all die."

"Do you want me to leave, dear?" Dohey asked.

"No, I want you to stay," muttered Cini.

"Then if you want me to stay, I'll stay."

"You're a fool for not going," Arpin told her as the plane left Great Falls for the second time that evening. "You should have left when you had the chance."

When the aircraft was well underway, this time towards Phoenix, Arizona, and not Regina as

The highjacked jet at the Calgary airport.

he had demanded earlier, Cini again changed his mind. He told Arpin to let the captain know they should fly to Calgary. Ehman agreed.

Then the already volatile hijacker became even more worked up. At one point, he accused the crew of piping lethal gas into the plane to kill him. On another occasion, he flew into a rage because he lit a cigarette and found that it was not his own brand. To ensure that this did not happen again, he ordered Dohey, Arpin and Bonné to sit down with him at the little table in the lounge.

When all four were seated, he took one cigarette from each of four packs, all different brands. He ordered Mary to light each and set them in an ashtray in the centre of the table. Then he turned the ashtray around and around, all the while telling his hostages that if the cigarette he selected from the ashtray was not his own, Mary would die.

He picked the right one and Mary Dohey almost collapsed with relief. "By this time, I was so tired, I almost gave up," she recalls.

As the big jet flew north, Cini embarked on yet another mad endeavour. He suddenly sprang to his feet and rushed into the cockpit.

"The next thing I knew," Dohey says, "he came marching out of the cockpit, behind the captain, with the shotgun aimed at the back of Vern's head. The captain was carrying all the radio headsets."

The two went down the centre aisle of the plane, back towards the now empty economy section. When they reached the tail section, Cini told

Ehman to open a door there, because he wanted to parachute out. Ehman refused, saying that opening the door would be impossible because of the slip stream. "Then I'll blow the back off the plane and jump out," Cini retorted.

Ehman dissuaded him, pointing out that if he really wanted to jump out, he could leave through one of the emergency windows over the wing. Cini agreed, but found that he could not open the window with one hand. When he set the shotgun down in order to free both his hands, Ehman saw his chance.

The pilot grabbed the shotgun and heaved it down the aisle. Then he lunged for Cini's throat, and at the same time yelled for help.

John Arpin raced to assist. Then Bonné and Dohey arrived. The four of them pinned Cini to the floor and he stopped struggling. Ehman said, "We've got to tie him up. Get some tape."

Captain Ehman shows how he grabbed hold of Cini.

Suddenly Cini went beserk. He threw them off and began to thrash around like a wild animal. Ehman grabbed the man's throat and the others fought to control him. They threw him down, but again he clambered to his feet.

"The axe, Phillip," Ehman yelled. "Hit him with the axe."

Phillip Bonné grabbed an emergency fire axe and belted Cini on the head with the blunt end. Cini shook off the blow and lunged at the captain. Bonné clouted him with the blade. Blood flew, but Cini was as ferocious as ever.

"Use the handle," yelled Ehman.

Bonné flipped the axe around, took the blade in both hands and brought the handle down.

There was a crunching sound, and the hijacker's body went limp. Arpin pulled off the hood Cini wore and they tied him down. Captain Ehman returned to the cockpit. Half an hour later, he brought Flight 812 down on the tarmac at Calgary — just 20 minutes before a heavy fog closed the airport for two days. It was now midnight, but the terrible ordeal was over.

*　　*　　*

Later, after he had recovered from his head wounds, Paul Joseph Cini was sent to prison. John Arpin, Vern Ehman, Phillip Bonné and Mary Dohey were all decorated for bravery, but Dohey alone received the Cross of Valour. She was the first person to win the award and live. She still flies for Air Canada.

Bob Teather

When the phone wakened him at four that morning, the policeman knew the call would be an emergency. He switched on his bedside light and answered the first ring. The voice on the line was familiar.

"Bob, listen closely," said the caller. "Rescue Coordination in Vancouver have just told me they have an overturned fishing boat with two men trapped inside it. They need a couple of divers right away. I'll pick you up in 10 minutes."

Then the line went dead.

Royal Canadian Mounted Police Corporal Robert Teather bounded out of bed, pulled a sweat-suit over his pajamas and told his wife Susan about the call.

"Not again!" she remarked. "Bob, be careful."

"Sure."

He kissed her on the cheek and dashed out of the room. Five minutes later, RCMP Dive Team supervisor, Corporal Tim Kain, pulled the police van into the driveway.

Teather tossed his diving gear in the rear door and ran around to the passenger side. He had hardly got into his seat when Kain tramped the accelerator and the vehicle shot into the darkened streets of Delta, British Columbia. "We have to meet a hovercraft at the government dock at Steveston," said Kain as he switched on the emergency lights and siren. "The sooner we get there, the better. Apparently the guys in the boat won't last long."

Teather says the drive from his home to the fishing village of Steveston was hair-raising. "It was a Code 3 — red lights and sirens all the way. Part of the trip was on a freeway, and when we swung off it we had a police escort the rest of the way. All the stop streets were cleared for us and we really flew. There isn't much traffic at 4:00 A.M., and we did the run in 18 minutes. In traffic it takes an hour."

As the divers were racing towards their destination, the two trapped fishermen managed to remain reasonably calm. They were boxed inside the inverted engine room of the little troller *Respond,* a 15-metre fishing boat that had capsized when it collided with the *Rimba Meranti,* a Malaysian lumber carrier on its way to Vancouver.

The accident happened shortly after 3:00 A.M. in the Strait of Georgia, some two kilometres out from the mouth of the Fraser River. A lookout on the freighter had failed to see the tiny white boat until it was too late to change course. The huge bulbous bow of the Malaysian ship had gone under the *Respond* and tossed it aside like a cork.

Initially, the captain of the fishing vessel, 24-year-old Rod Larden, thought his boat had hit a submerged log. But then, as the *Respond* began to list further and further and failed to right herself, he realized what had happened. By the time the little boat was on its side, Larden and 23-year-old

Frank Michelanko, the second man on board, along with Larden's black Labrador dog Tiki, were all bracing themselves for what was coming.

Within seconds, the *Respond* was upside down, with the two men and the dog lying on the ceiling of the wheelhouse. For a brief time the place was dry, but then torrents of water began rushing in. Tiki sensed the danger even more quickly than the men. She began to whine, and in her terror, looked for safety.

Looking up from the engine room where the *Respond*'s crew were trapped.

Rod glanced above him in the direction of the surface. Now however, the only thing farther up was the engine room. He scrambled into it, and as he did, heaved Tiki up with him. The dog was shaking with fear.

Frank was not a swimmer, and the swiftly rising water drove him to the edge of panic. He had picked himself up as soon as the boat became stable, but then had watched in horror as the water rose — first to his knees, then to his waist and shoulders.

Rod yelled from above, urged Frank to climb, and extended a hand to bring his friend to safety. The task was not easy. Michelanko weighed over 90 kilograms, while Larden was slight, about 30 kilograms lighter. Nevertheless, Michelanko succeeded in getting up to the engine room seconds before the wheelhouse became totally submerged. As it did, Rod grabbed an emergency flashlight.

It was not until both men were actually in the engine room that they realized the motor was still running. When Rod reached to shut it off, hot oil gushed over his neck and shoulders. He pulled back with a start.

Then the lights went out.

The sudden darkness was as unexpected as it was eerie. For a period, neither man spoke, and although she whimpered once or twice, even Tiki became still. The claustrophobic silence was overwhelming.

On the surface, the *Rimba Meranti* immediately radioed the Canadian Coast Guard and told them of the collision. The coast guard, in turn, broadcast a distress call to ships that might be in the area of the mishap. Two that were close enough sped to the scene and offered to help in any way they could.

The first requirement was lighting. Because the accident had happened in pitch darkness — there was no moonlight — the floating hull of the upturned fishing vessel was no more than a dark object on a black sea. The lights and the motor had died, and the first persons to arrive on the scene surmised that the occupants of the boat were dead as well. Attempts to communicate with anyone proved futile, both by loud-hailer and by radio, and there had been no Mayday broadcast.

When they were unable to learn the fate of the *Respond's* crew, the four men on the *Tsonoqua*, the first vessel to reach the scene, decided to pull their boat up beside the *Respond*. As they did, they kept yelling.

Down inside the hull of the upturned ship, the men and the dog in the oily hell heard a sound. Larden switched on his flashlight. Tiki sat up, stopped shivering and yelped.

Silence.

Then the sound outside came again. Michelanko and Larden looked at each other, and their beaming faces said there might be hope. Rod grabbed a wrench, pounded on the aluminum hull and listened.

"Is there anybody there?" came a muffled voice from outside. "Is there anybody there?"

Larden pounded again and Tiki barked. "Yes, two of us," shouted Larden, "and my dog."

"Good. We'll try to help you," said the voice.

The *Tsonoqua* stood by, and a coast guard hovercraft arrived. As soon as the skipper of the hovercraft learned that men were alive inside the fishing boat, he radioed for divers, spun his craft around and sped towards Steveston for Tim Kain and Bob Teather. But as his machine raced over the 15 kilometres to get them, he found himself wondering if they would ever be able to save the men in that sunken hull. He knew the pocket of air under the *Respond* would not be there for long.

"There were four crewmen on the hovercraft when it met us," recalls Bob Teather today. "The captain, a navigator and two others. As well, a couple of policemen left their cruiser and helped us load the diving gear, oxygen resuscitators and so on. This job generally takes at least 20 minutes. That night it was completed in five.

"The trip out to the boat took about 15 minutes because the hovercraft they were using cruises at close to 80 kilometres an hour. The sea was rolling slightly, and I don't recall any stars. You could see a few lights from Vancouver, away off in the distance. Tim and I started to put on our diving suits as we went along."

During this interval, a small tugboat reached the accident scene and the tug's captain turned a couple of floodlights on the *Respond*. Since voice communication had also been established, for a time the situation seemed more hopeful. But then the men waiting for the police divers learned that it would probably be difficult to use whatever escape route might be below. Larden had attempted to hold his breath and dive down under his floating prison, but he was unable to open a jammed door that blocked the passageway leading outside. He had been driven back to the engine room as the *Respond* settled lower and lower. By the time the coast guard hovercraft arrived, the air pocket was no bigger than the interior of a compact car.

"The hovercraft skipper slowed down as we came up to the scene," says Teather, "because we didn't want to jostle the fishing boat too much. At that stage, no one knew how much air was underneath. When we were settled in the water and the big searchlights from the hovercraft were switched on, the place was quite bright.

"Tim and I were in our diving suits by this time, but we didn't have our diving tanks on yet. When the forward hatch of the hovercraft was lowered, we walked down the gangplank to the edge of the water. That was when the enormity of the whole thing hit me.

"We looked over at the upturned hull and I thought of the poor guys down inside it. I knew right then that whoever went down for them would likely never come out alive. It really terrified me. After we both looked on in silence for a second or two, Tim put his hand on my shoulder and said, 'My God, this is not a drill.' I felt sick."

As soon as he was close enough to the *Respond* to touch it, Teather took his diver's knife and scratched a long mark on the ship's hull, just at the water line. "I knew it was going to be a few minutes before we went in, and I wanted to see what the boat was doing. Ten minutes later, when my mark was 15 centimetres lower in the water, I knew time was running out. The boat was sinking. On top of that, the wind was picking up and the sea was becoming choppy.

"I needed to know as much about the situation as I could, so I climbed up on the hull and asked the guys inside three questions: 'Do you speak English?' 'How many are there?' and "Is anybody hurt?' I wanted to know if I could talk to them, and if I *did* get inside, I wanted some idea of what I could expect. Their answers were muffled, but by putting your ear close to the hull, you could hear pretty well.

"Then Tim and I put on our tanks, masks and fins and swam down under the *Respond* to see what things were like. The whole place was a real mess. There were fishing lines all over the place, hanging down and more or less drifting with the current. There was also a lot of debris and patches of oily scum, and that made it hard to see very far.

"We had hand lanterns, and with the light we managed to locate a Dutch door leading to the passageway down the centre of the boat. The door itself was in two sections, so that ordinarily the top could be opened, or both parts could be. Anyway, one half wouldn't budge, so we knew if we were able to get the guys out it would be a tight squeeze. That was when we realized only one of us could do the dive. There would not be room for both."

The two divers surfaced. The first thing they noticed was that the sea was rougher now and the wind stronger than it had been. An earlier suggestion that a hole be cut into the hull of the *Respond* so the fishermen could escape was tossed aside as impractical. The boat would go down like a rock if the air pocket was disturbed. But now almost everyone on the scene knew that, air pocket or not, rough water might soon sink the ailing craft.

"When Tim and I realized how bad things actually were, we looked at each other and decided I would be the one to go down. Tim would stay in the water and take the men from me if I could get them out. At this stage, I really did not want to do the dive. I honestly felt I'd never come out. However, I also believe that when you decide to be a cop you are expected to put your life on the line if necessary. That comes with the territory."

The divers worked feverishly on last-minute preparations for what lay ahead. The pressure regulator at the top of Kain's diving tank was cannibalized and Teather's tank was rigged in such a way that it would have an extra breathing apparatus. Then Teather slid into the water and the rescue attempt began. It was 5:40 A.M.

"I spent a short time tying the fishing lines out of the way," he recalls. "I knew that if I did get one or both of the men we could drown just by getting tangled up on our way out.

"Once I had the lines tied, I tried to open the other half of the Dutch door, but still got nowhere. Finally, I swam in through the open half and immediately got lost. I had a light with me, but there was almost no visibility. There was a lot of oil and gasoline in the water, but as well, the whole passageway was obscured by hundreds of bits of soggy dog kibble.

"There was a small anteroom just inside the

Dutch door, and that was where I got lost. I did a couple of turnarounds somehow, but finally got back to the door and started over. This time I swam along the floor, which was my ceiling. There were cupboard doors open and junk all over the place, so I tried to clear a passage as I went. Then I felt something hit my head."

By this time, Larden, Michelanko and Tiki were confined in the tiniest of spaces. Nevertheless, Larden was able to shine his flashlight into the murky water as a guide for Teather. But because the policeman was facing away from the light and didn't see it, Larden hit him on the head with a broomstick and guided him to the air pocket.

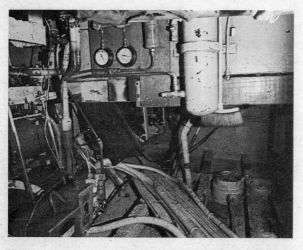

The life-saving air pocket was at the bottom of the overturned boat (top half of this photo).

A second later, the trapped fishermen saw the man who represented their only hope of getting out alive.

"Hi there," chirped Teather when he came face to face with the two. "How are you?"

"My first thought was that these guys were really cool after what they'd been through," he recalls. "We had a brief, two-second conversation and then I asked who was going first."

"He is," Larden answered. "I'm the skipper. Frank goes first."

Teather said, "Okay, Frank, get in the water and I'll teach you how to dive."

Michelanko apparently thought the mountie was standing on something.

"He moved over beside me," explains Teather, "and the next thing I knew we were both under the water. I didn't know he couldn't swim, and I guess he grabbed me to steady himself. We both went under and I swallowed some oil. There was a five-centimetre film of oil, gasoline and kibble on the top of the water, so everything you touched was slimy. When I finally got Frank back up where I wanted him, I threw up."

Teather wiped the oil from the oxygen mouth-piece and showed Frank what to do next.

"I breathed through one and he used the other. Then I told him to hold the mouthpiece in with his right hand, and to place his left on my tank belt, at the nape of my neck."

Michelanko did as he was told.

"Now, Frank," Teather continued, "hold on tight and I'll take you out on my back."

The big man nodded.

The two ducked under the water and started down towards the engine room hatch that opened in the floor of the central passageway. They managed to squeeze through the hatch, but then the confined space, the darkness, and the fact that he could not swim got to Michelanko. He panicked.

The fisherman began to flail around, out of control. He wrapped his legs around Teather's waist and grabbed the slim, 68-kilogram policeman around the neck. Teather lost his mask and his oxygen mouthpiece. The two tumbled over and over in the tiny, underwater chamber, and Teather's lungs ached for air. He choked on the oily water and kibble and began retching as he desperately attempted to get his bearings and find his mouthpiece. Each time he threw up, the involuntary contraction of his throat caused him to suck in more of the putrid water around him.

Finally, luckily, the mountie was able to locate the missing oxygen line.

"I jammed it back into my mouth," he recalls with a shudder, "but I was still without my mask and I had to let the light I carried go because I needed both hands just to get the mouthpiece back in and try to steady myself. Frank was still clutched to me, so I opened my eyes to see if I could tell where we were.

"All I could see was a faint, greenish glow, which I knew must be coming from the floodlights outside. I went into a fetal position and Frank's grip was not so tight. Somehow, we got to the Dutch door, but I really don't know how we ever got through it. I do know the squeeze was really tight and Frank must have felt like a barnacle being scraped off the bottom of a boat. Anyway, he held on and I remember bracing my feet against the door sill and pushing myself towards the surface.

"Because I couldn't see very well, I came up on the far side of the boat, away from the hovercraft. When we got to the surface, I went into the fetal position again in order to ease Frank's hold on me. Then I screamed for help, and in 10 seconds Tim Kain was beside me, prying Frank off my back. The gasoline had burned Frank's eyes and he couldn't see, and I don't think he knew where we were. He and Tim struggled a bit, but Tim was able to get him to the hovercraft."

Teather rested in the water for a few seconds before getting ready to go down for Larden.

"I had trouble getting everything together," he says, "because whatever I touched had a film of oil over it. My mask had been looped around my neck, under the oxygen line, so it had to be wiped off. As I was doing this, Tim swam back to me and asked how I was. He said he would go for the second man, but I told him there wasn't time."

With that, Teather popped his mouthpiece back in and dived for the Dutch door. A minute later he was in the engine room talking to Larden.

"Okay, Rod, you're next."

"What about Tiki?" asked Larden. "Take Tiki first, I'll wait."

"No, I want to take you now, Rod. I'll come back for Tiki," Teather responded.

The second fisherman grasped Teather and the two drifted down, out of the engine room. This time the rescue went as planned. Teather was able to maintain his direction, and Larden floated out with relative ease. Tim Kain met them on the surface and hoisted Larden from the water.

When he saw that the second man was safe, Teather told Kain that Tiki was next.

"Oh no, she isn't," Kain retorted. "You've done enough." He grabbed Teather's harness and hauled his friend to safety.

Up on the hovercraft the crew was cheering.

*   *   *

Several hours after the accident, the *Respond* was towed to shore and another diver went to the engine room for Tiki. He brought her out alive. On Friday, June 24, 1983, Bob Teather received the Cross of Valour and Tim Kain the Medal of Bravery for their heroics in the rescue of Larden and Michelanko.

Gaston Langelier

Laval Maximum Security Institution, just north of Montreal, is a jail housing some of the most notorious criminals in Canada. Here, in the sprawling, granite fortress that was once called St. Vincent de Paul Penitentiary, 500 men live, work, sleep and dream of being free. Few of them are pleasant people, and all are here because they have broken the law.

The prison was built more than 100 years ago and received its first inmates on May 20, 1873. Since then it has been enlarged, modernized, renamed, but rarely praised. Indeed, the complex has been found wanting during most of its infamous history. In 1973 it was condemned and closed, but a short while later had to be reopened because of an increase in prison population.

This institution, like so many others, houses lawbreakers of all kinds: murderers, rapists, drug dealers and thieves. And while they may all be different, in one way at least they are all the same: they all want to get out.

Over the years, a number of convicts have escaped from Laval. Some were away for a few hours, others for a few days. A few were never recaptured. On the whole, however, most were eventually caught. But the knowledge that escapees are usually caught has never been much of a deterrent to those who want to break out. Certainly it was no deterrent to the five men who planned to escape in the early afternoon of Tuesday, July 11, 1978.

The five, Jacques Massey (35), Pierre Vincent (33), André Chartrand (23), Ghislain Gaudette (27) and Jean Lachapelle (41) were all serving time for either armed robbery or murder. All had been in the prison for some time, and all were considered dangerous. One of the five, Vincent, had escaped several times from several jails. He thrived on doing so.

At 1:00 P.M. on the day of the escape, the electronically operated steel doors from the cell blocks swung open to permit the inmates to enter the cavernous central square, or "dome" of Laval. From here, the prisoners moved to various other locations within the penitentiary itself. Some reported for work. Others went to see lawyers. Some had visitors, and as always, a few reported to the medical ward. The five men who planned to escape

carried written passes to see prison officials. These passes were forged.

The five proceeded separately through the dome, across the paved prison grounds towards the guarded entrance to the two-storey administration wing of the jail. This 200-metre walk was witnessed by armed guards on duty in the observation towers, high above the prison walls. None of them noticed anything amiss.

Even though the five had not walked together to the administration wing, they did come together at the entrance to it. This stratagem was deliberate. The first two showed their passes to Richard Rolland, a security guard inside a steel-reinforced control booth just outside the administration vestibule. Rolland checked the passes and signalled to Marc Drouin, a second guard stationed in the vestibule, to open the door to permit the two inmates to enter.

The first part of the escape plan was working.

The door was hardly open before all five convicts charged through it. Drouin stumbled backwards in surprise, and the next thing he knew, both he and a male nurse who happened to be with him were forced against the opposite wall by the inmates holding deadly, sharpened stilettos or "pics."

One of the convicts told Drouin and the nurse to do as they were told and they would not be harmed. Another, Jacques Massey, reached into his trousers pocket and produced a small .25 calibre handgun that had been smuggled into the prison. He pointed the weapon at Rolland, the guard, and ordered him to open the security cage and hand out a revolver and a shotgun that were inside.

Rolland refused.

Massey flew into a rage, pushed his pistol through a small opening into the control booth and fired three shots, the first of which passed through Rolland's body, wounding him seriously. The other two shots hit the corner of a desk and the arm of the chair where Rolland had been sitting. Despite his injuries, the guard managed to drag himself under his desk, out of the line of fire. Because of his wounds, he was unable to do anything further to impede the escape.

The volley of shots seemed to drive all five prisoners into a frenzy. Because they had been frustrated in their attempts to obtain more weapons, they turned to Marc Drouin, ripped his keys from his belt and managed to open the door that led from the vestibule into the second-floor office area. Massey then grabbed Drouin by the collar, jammed the pistol into the small of his back and ordered him to cooperate. Drouin realized that he was being used as a shield and expected to be shot if the escape attempt was interrupted. He did as he was told. The male nurse was left in the vestibule.

There are several offices and some 30 doorways leading off the long hallway on the second floor of the administration wing. Halfway down the hall is a sliding steel grille barrier that can be secured to prevent escape. One of the escapees raced down the hall and propped a chair into the open barrier to keep it from closing. Three others went from office to office, using the pics to threaten people and ordering everyone they found into the hall. Massey held his gun on Marc Drouin.

As each office was vacated, the crowd of terrified hostages grew larger. The inmates screamed at everyone to hurry, and the grim procession moved swiftly towards the large conference room and adjoining stairs leading down to the main entrance of the prison. Just before the stairs, on the left, is the office of the assistant director of security. At the time of the escape, this person was Gaston Langelier.

"I had been in the correctional service for 23 years," he recalls, "and I had been at Laval for three. I had had experience with other escapes, but this one was by far the most serious for me.

"I was sitting at my desk when I heard some racket in the hall outside. The next thing I knew, inmate Massey barged into my office, put his revolver up to my head and ordered me out into the corridor. By this time, there were 20 or 30 people there. I did what he asked."

While this was happening, one of the hostages, who was ahead of the others, raced down the stairs and passed through a swing-open grille barrier at the bottom. He yelled for the front door of the prison to be opened because he feared for the lives of the hostages who were coming behind him. Already some of them were at the top of the stairs.

The first person to hear the plea was 27-year-old Guy Fournier, a guard on duty at the main desk. He immediately ran to investigate. As he got to the grille barrier, he was met by several fleeing employees. Fournier jumped to the side and the crowd swept past. He glanced up the stairs, just as Gaston Langelier and another officer, Marcel Boucher, were coming down. Behind the two was an inmate with a gun.

"I was on the left side, facing down," says Langelier. "Marcel Boucher was on my right and Jacques Massey was walking behind us. At this time, Massey had the gun in the back of Mr. Boucher and was pushing me with his hand. Then, out of the corner of my eye, I noticed the inmate make a move to take the revolver with his other hand. That was when I went for him."

Suddenly, Langelier spun around, grabbed Massey by the arm and twisted it up behind the convict's back. The inmate cursed, ducked his head and lurched across the stairs. The gun clattered onto the terrazzo steps and the two men fell, both wildly grasping for the weapon. At this point there was a lot of shouting and Langelier and Massey tumbled to the bottom of the stairs. As he fell, Langelier shouted for the barrier to be closed.

For a split second, the gun lay by itself.

Guard Guy Fournier saw it first. He dashed to retrieve it, but inmate Lachapelle was quicker. He grabbed the weapon, brought it up to chest level and fired one shot. Fournier was hit in the forehead and died within seconds. Marc Drouin, the 21-year-old guard who had been the first hostage taken, lunged at Lachapelle, apparently to stop him from shooting at Fournier. Instead, the inmate turned to face the young guard and fired a second time. The bullet ripped into Drouin's jaw, spun him around and caused him to fall down the stairs. Later, he was able to get to his feet and leave with the last of the hostages.

"As the two shots rang out, there was a great deal of shouting and screaming," Gaston Langelier remembers. "Then I could see that another officer at the control post by the main entrance was trying to hand me a gun. I guess Lachapelle saw the same thing, because he came over and took charge of me. He had his gun in my back and then he started screaming at somebody to open the front door or there would be a massacre."

While Langelier was being held by Lachapelle with the gun, guard Boucher and others were threatened by the convicts holding the sharpened pics. The situation just inside the front doors was becoming more frenzied, with much screaming, shoving and crying. Finally someone, and no one knows who, ordered the door to the main lobby opened.

As soon as the pressure was off, a torrent of terrified humanity poured through. Both employees and convicts raced for the exit, and once through it, fled in panic away from the deadly chaos at the foot of the stairs.

"There were people all over the place," says Langelier. "Convicts, visitors who were there to see inmates, other hostages . . . Then, when the doors opened, everyone tried to get out at once — including Lachapelle and the other inmates.

"As soon as he saw the open door, Lachapelle

forgot about me, but I grabbed him because I was determined he was not going to get away. Then he shot me."

When Langelier moved to stop the fleeing convict, Lachapelle raised his weapon and fired twice. Both shots hit the assistant security director on the right side of his face and propelled him across the room towards the front entrance control post.

"I knew he was going to shoot again," says Langelier with a shudder, "and I was sure I was going to be killed. But then I saw the door guard push the .38 towards me through the small opening in his control post. As I was about to grab the gun to defend myself, another bullet broke my arm. I kept going, something like the walking dead. I knew I was bleeding a lot because I saw my reflection in the control post glass. Blood was spurting from my ear.

"Anyway, I finally managed to grab the revolver, and when I turned around, Lachapelle was shooting at me from across the room. I fired back and he shot again and again — from three metres away. I felt as though I was dying, and then I saw him fall. He died in the lobby.

"Somehow I kept going. I handed the gun back and walked on my own to another room called the Keeper's Hall. As soon as I got there, they put me on a couch and called an ambulance. They also gave me the last rites of the Catholic Church."

In the meantime, on the floor above, a woman who had been in a washroom during the roundup of the hostages crept from her hiding place and glanced down the corridor towards the stairs. When she knew she was out of sight, she darted into her office and phoned guards in the dome and towers to alert them of the escape in progress. Other areas of the prison were immediately secured.

By this time the escapees had left Lachapelle behind and were out the front door. They extricated themselves from the mob of panic-stricken employees, raced across the jail parking lot, and surrounded a red Toyota that had just pulled onto the property.

One of the convicts yelled at the driver, Jean Vigneault, pushed him into the back seat and placed a pic against his neck. Then the other three climbed into the little car, rammed it into gear and raced across a front lawn and off the property. As they sped north on Montée St-François, shots rang out from the towers atop the prison, but none was accurate. Later, Vigneault was released unharmed.

* * *

The daring, bloody daylight escape from Laval was over. In its aftermath, two men were dead — a guard and a convict. Three other guards were injured, but all of them, including Gaston Langelier, recovered successfully. Marc Drouin, the first hostage, and Guy Fournier, the murdered guard, were both awarded the Star of Courage, the nation's second highest award for bravery. Eight months after the incident, Gaston Langelier received the Cross of Valour. He still works for the Correctional Service of Canada.

Subsequently, all the escapees were captured.

Amedeo Garrammone

Shortly after 10:00 P.M. on November 4, 1978, three young sailors finished their meal, left a tip on the table, paid their bill and stepped out into Gottingen Street in the north end of Halifax, Nova Scotia. Although the evening was cool, the fog and rain of earlier days had at least gone. That night the weather, like the mood of the three, was decidedly pleasant.

They had spent most of that Saturday together, and had decided earlier in the evening to go out for a late snack. All three were stationed at Canadian Forces Base Halifax, and the restaurant they went to was just across the street from the main gates. They had eaten at Venus Pizza before, and they not only liked the food, they also liked the people who ran the place. Moreover, the service was fast and the prices were right.

As the three friends waited for the traffic to clear before they crossed the street to return to their barracks, they noticed a tall, sandy-haired, rather unkempt-looking young man standing in the shadows nearby. A woman was with him.

The man shouted something at the sailors, but they ignored him. "Hey, goof," he yelled, this time loudly and with a good deal of sarcastic belligerence. "Hey, goof, come here!" he repeated, glaring at 18-year-old Bradley Quinn from Hamilton, Ontario.

Brad Quinn turned.

Then the man, whose name was Stuart "Skippy" Hamblin, slowly removed his jacket, handed it to the woman and walked over to Quinn.

Quinn didn't move.

Hamblin snarled something else, positioned himself directly in front of Quinn and punched the young sailor in the face. The punch had hardly landed when Quinn decided he had taken enough. His right hand flashed. Then his left. Then his right again. Hamblin muttered an obscenity, tried to duck his head and finally crumpled in a heap on the pavement. The fight was over.

Stephen Holden, one of the navy men with Quinn, stepped forward and took his friend's shoulder. As he did so, Hamblin got to his feet and raced towards the Northend Beverage Room, a nearby hotel. The woman was left behind.

For a few seconds James Hoy, the third sailor, along with Holden and Quinn, stood and watched Hamblin run. Then Hoy turned to cross the street, this time slightly ahead of his two friends. Quinn glanced in the direction of the hotel, but then, following some urging from Holden, shrugged his shoulders and started back towards the base.

Skippy Hamblin, an ex-convict who had just been released from prison after serving time for crimes of violence, was not about to lose face. He had been defeated and embarrassed in public, in a fight he had started, and he now wanted to get even. To his mind, whether he got even in a fair way or not did not matter. Unfortunately for Brad Quinn, the method Hamblin chose did matter. Although he thought the affair ended, Brad Quinn would soon die.

James Hoy had just crossed the street when he heard some commotion in front of the hotel. He turned to his left and noticed Skippy Hamblin and two other men barge into the street, pause for a second or two, then start to run towards Brad. Quinn noticed them as well, but apparently decided he had had enough fighting. He dashed towards the main entrance of Stadacona, the Halifax Canadian Forces Base.

As he did, he ran past a man proceeding in the same direction. This man was Amedeo Garrammone.

Earlier that evening, jovial, 23-year-old Garrammone, a champion weight-lifter in the Canadian military, had gone for a walk downtown. He was wearing a light shirt and slacks and a brown corduroy jacket. "The jacket was not particularly heavy," he says today, "so when the evening started to get cooler, I decided to turn back to the base. As I was approaching Stadacona, I was walking fairly fast, but suddenly a tall young guy with short, dark hair raced past me. Three guys were chasing him.

"From the look of things, I was pretty sure there was going to be a fight," Garrammone recalls, "but I had no idea what it was about. I knew none of the people involved. From the way the first guy was running, though, I figured he would make it to the front gates of the base without getting caught. He was really flying."

While his friends watched from some distance back along the street, Brad Quinn steadily drew away from his pursuers. Two of them were already falling behind, and Skippy Hamblin was even farther back.

Suddenly, Quinn's right foot came down on a loose stone on the sidewalk. He stumbled, then lurched sideways and fell face down on the cement. He had just got back on his feet when the two strangers reached him.

"The next thing I knew, they were both beating the fellow who ran past me," says Garrammone. "They were punching him and kicking him and he was up against a wall and couldn't get away. Then the third guy got there and he seemed to dance up and down for a couple seconds, as if he was waiting his turn."

After the two men with Hamblin had delivered several blows, Hamblin apparently decided his chance had come. But instead of using his fists, or even his feet, he reached under his clothing and pulled out a knife. Then he lunged at Quinn with it.

"I saw him raise his left hand," Garrammone recounts, "and then I saw the blade flash for a second in the light from a streetlamp overhead. The hand came down again and again, and I knew the guy against the wall was being stabbed."

Garrammone stood transfixed for a second, almost disbelieving what he was seeing. The hand with the knife was swinging wildly, while the young sailor being struck moaned in pain and vainly tried to protect himself. "No! No more. Please, no more," he cried, but Hamblin continued his insane assault.

Garrammone recovered his senses, yelled at the attackers and rushed to the scene.

"I really was hoping somebody would help me," he says today. "I looked across at the west side of Gottingen Street and thought I saw several sailors on the sidewalk in front of the hotel. One man started towards the fight, but he seemed to stop in the middle of the street.

"By the time I reached the location, the thug with the knife was really going at it. I yelled at him to stop and grabbed him by the shoulders.

"We scuffled for a few seconds and he was cursing me. Then he swung around and attacked me from the right. I tried to break the speed of his hand but I was not able to do so. The knife penetrated the right side of my chest and the tip went across and into my heart.

"At that time I straightened up and looked straight into his eyes, while the knife was still in my chest. We stayed like that for about two seconds, but then I seemed to become paralyzed and I couldn't carry on the fight any longer.

"When he pulled the blade out, blood gushed out of my chest and I put my hand over the wound. When the knife went in, I felt no physical pain, but as soon as it was out and I was losing blood, I started to lose strength."

As soon as he realized that Garrammone was out of action, Hamblin turned again to Quinn. He stabbed the fallen sailor three more times, but then was pulled off by his fellow attackers. "Let's go, Skippy!" shouted one of them, and the three dashed away. The whole incident lasted less than a minute.

While Quinn lay bleeding on the sidewalk, Amedeo Garrammone staggered towards the main gate at Stadacona, 20 metres away.

"Every move I made took a lot out of me," he winces, "but I kept telling myself I didn't want to die. An old man came towards me and asked what had happened. I don't know if I told him or not. At the main gate, the duty commissionaire looked at me but didn't seem to know what was wrong.

"I felt my knees becoming weak, and I was trying to tell him I had been stabbed and there was another man on the sidewalk, but not much sound was coming out of my throat. I felt that my tongue was going down my throat, choking me. I put one knee on the cement and bent over because the pain was burning in my chest, but I refused to fall until I could hold out no more. Finally, I guess I fell over.

"The next thing I knew, there seemed to be a lot of people running around me, shouting, and I was pointing at my mouth, trying to get somebody

These bloodstains on the sidewalk were located just in front of the nearest pole in the photo above.

to give me air. Later, I was told that a military policeman put a ruler in my mouth and kept me from swallowing my tongue. I was sweating a cold sweat, and then everything was darkness."

By the time his horrified friends realized what had happened, Brad Quinn was lying on the sidewalk with 18 stab wounds in his upper body. The two ran to Quinn's side and screamed for an ambulance. One of them attempted to pursue Hamblin, but thought better of it. The man was vicious and he still had the knife. Instead, they bent over their friend and tried to comfort him until help arrived. But already Brad Quinn was dying.

An ambulance arrived quickly, but the medical officer who helped load Quinn noticed that his breathing was already forced. The trip to the hospital lasted 90 seconds, during which time ambulance personnel massaged the victim's chest and applied mouth-to-mouth resuscitation. The efforts were futile, however. Dr. John Hamilton, on duty at the base hospital that night, pronounced Brad Quinn dead two minutes after his arrival in emergency.

Eight minutes passed from the time Garrammone was stabbed until the ambulance was able to return for him. During this time he lay on his back, bled profusely and fought to stay alive. A small crowd gathered, but the military and city police moved the curious onlookers away from the scene. The police also began to record names of witnesses to the stabbings. One name they obtained was that of Antonio LaChance, a Halifax taxi driver.

Just as the assailants were running after

Quinn, LaChance was parking his taxi across the street. He saw the chase, and he also saw Hamblin using the knife to stab Quinn. When Hamblin fled, the cab driver followed in his car. A block away from the scene of the murder, LaChance caught sight of Hamblin, who was walking swiftly down a side street. As LaChance approached from the rear, he noticed that Hamblin still carried the knife.

The cab driver lowered a window, yelled at Hamblin and mentioned the knife. Hamblin cursed, ducked behind the cab and disappeared down an alley. As soon as he realized he had lost his quarry, LaChance swung his vehicle around and went to report what he had seen to the police. In the meantime, ambulance attendants were wheeling Garrammone into the hospital where Brad Quinn had just died.

"I remember opening my eyes at the hospital," Garrammone says today. "I saw the ceiling in the emergency ward, but not much else. I asked a nurse about the man who was stabbed and she told me he had passed away. Then I gave somebody my girlfriend's phone number and I told them to call her. My own family wasn't in Halifax, and I didn't want them to know I was in the hospital. I knew they would worry."

Garrammone has a few isolated memories of what was done to him during his first evening in the hospital:

"I remember lying there and a surgeon telling me to roll over. Then a nurse told me to breathe deeply into a mask. Then I was out.

"During the operation I remember fighting hard to stay alive because I was somehow aware that something was going wrong. I felt as though my head was diving in one direction and my feet were going the other way — and at that time I could hear a lot of noise in the room.

"Then I became very frightened and I wanted to scream, but I was terribly tired and I couldn't move. I never felt so bad in all my life. That was when I decided to let myself go. As soon as I did, I felt no more fear but felt warm and good. There were lots of lights. When I woke up later in intensive care, I was actually kind of disappointed. I can't explain why."

Amedeo Garrammone was born in Belgium, the son of an Italian coalminer who also sang opera. There are seven children in the family, and at the time of the Halifax stabbing, the family was living in Montreal. Both parents speak Italian and French.

"The Roman Catholic padre contacted my parents," says Garrammone now. "They flew to Halifax, and my girlfriend, Eve Galley, met them. She had never seen them before, and when they arrived she had to hold up a sign at the airport with my name on it. They came over to her, of course, but because she couldn't speak their languages, she couldn't tell them if I was alive or dead. She took my mother's hand and squeezed it, and they drove to the hospital in silence."

*　　*　　*

Amedeo Garrammone was in the hospital for three weeks and off work for two months. He is now a police officer in the Canadian Forces and has recently returned from an overseas posting at the Canadian Embassy in Beirut, Lebanon.

His assailant, Stuart Hamblin, was apprehended by the Halifax police and charged with the second degree murder of Brad Quinn. After a six-day trial that saw a total of 29 witnesses take the stand, an all-male jury found the defendant guilty as charged. He was sent to prison for life.

Ken Bishop

On the second last day of March, 1974, 43-year-old James McAdie was driving a fully loaded fuel truck east along Highway 16 in central Alberta. Hooked behind his rig was a pup trailer, also loaded. The afternoon was warm, the arrow-straight road was dry, and McAdie's spirits were as bright as the sun that shone overhead.

Despite the reasonably heavy Saturday traffic out of Edmonton, he was making good time, and at 1:45 P.M. was about 15 kilometres west of the Ukrainian settlement of Vegreville. As he hauled his 55 000 litres of diesel fuel across the prairie, he looked out at the snow-covered fields, dazzling in their brilliance. The hum of tires on blacktop was pleasant, and the vehicle he drove was working well. At least, it *had* been working well. Up ahead, perhaps half a kilometre away, he noticed another truck coming towards him.

The approaching transport, carrying 20 tonnes of flour, was driven by Robert Warren Hunter, 25, of Saskatoon.

Bob Hunter was born in St. Boniface, Manitoba, but when he was 11 he moved with his parents to Saskatoon. There he went to St. Philip Elementary School and later completed his secondary education at Saskatoon Technical. He spent one year in the army, but decided to return to civilian life and drive transports. In his spare time he loved to race stock cars. Hunter was married and had a little daughter.

A short distance behind Hunter's semi-trailer was a pickup truck carrying three people: 19-year-old Leslie Ferguson from Innisfail, Alberta, and Kay Green and her daughter Janice, who lived in nearby Vegreville.

Following after the pickup were several vehicles, spaced at various distances, stretching back halfway to Vegreville. Somewhere in the midst of these was a car driven by 28-year-old Ken Bishop, a soft-spoken, rather reserved young man who resided at the time in Lloydminster, on the Alberta-Saskatchewan border. Ken Bishop also drove trucks for a living.

The traffic was moving at a constant speed, as if no one was in a hurry to be somewhere else. Few drivers attempted to pass.

Up in the cab of his oil tanker, Jim McAdie glanced at his watch and reasoned that he would be in Vegreville before 2:00 P.M. From there, the road was good; there were no hills and few curves all the way to the Saskatchewan border. The highway itself was two-lane, seven metres across, with wide, shallow ditches. Just beyond the north ditch was a railway.

As McAdie's glance shifted back to the road in front of him, he noted that the approaching transport was less than 100 metres away. He flashed his headlights and the other driver returned the greeting. As they were about to meet, both drivers waved.

That wave was Bob Hunter's last.

Suddenly, and without any warning, the steering mechanism on the fuel tanker broke. Jim McAdie grabbed the wheel and wrenched it to one side, but the instrument spun in his hands. His truck was out of control!

The huge, powerful vehicles came closer and closer together. McAdie automatically tramped his brakes and in the same instant hit the horn. The truck was veering to the left.

Bob Hunter gaped in open-mouthed horror as the speeding tanker roared down on him, its front end two metres across the centre line of the road. He yanked his steering wheel to the right in a desperate attempt to avoid a crash. He did not have time to use his brakes. The last thing he saw was the grille of the truck that would kill him.

A split second later, the inevitable happened.

With a sickening roar, the vehicles tore into each other, sending a monstrous, ear-splitting crash echoing across the snowswept plains. Metal was torn like paper. The big, labouring diesel engines broke apart like tenpins hit by a bowling ball. Broken glass, chunks of plastic, rubber and steel flew in every direction. The massive machines, locked in a deadly embrace, grated to one side and came to rest half in and half out of the north ditch. Choking exhaust, steam from ruptured radiators, clouds of dust and stifling diesel fumes swirled across the wrecks. McAdie's tanker broke open and thousands of litres of fuel spewed everywhere. The pup-trailer he had been hauling ruptured on the road.

Robert Hunter was crushed in his cab, his hands still clutching the wheel. James McAdie was alive — yet.

When the transport hit, McAdie was torn from his seat, propelled through the windshield and thrown into the debris by the road. His right leg was almost severed and the force of the impact left him in shock, on his side, half-conscious from the searing pain, lying in a lake of oil.

The pickup that had been following Hunter's truck was unable to stop in time and crashed into the rear of the flour transport. All three occupants of the smaller vehicle were injured, but none seriously.

In rapid succession, cars and trucks approaching from either direction stopped, their occupants hardly believing what they saw. No other driver drove into the wrecks, but there were several close calls as the traffic ground to a halt. Within a minute or two several motorists rushed to the scene of the crash. It was obvious there would be people in trouble. They assisted the occupants of the pickup truck, and once it was apparent that they were in reasonably good shape, went to look for the transport drivers.

Jim McAdie was found right away, but when the onlookers saw his plight, they backed off. His mangled leg bothered some people, but even more alarming was his precarious position on the shoulder of the road. The trucker lay on a tiny ridge between the edge of the pavement and the ditch. He seemed dazed, as if he was not sure what had happened. Around him, on all sides, was a river of diesel fuel. Most who saw it understood, instinctively, that the slightest spark would cause the liquid to ignite — and if it did, the poor man on the ground would surely perish.

Yet in all the confusion, no one *did* anything, mainly because no one knew what to do.

McAdie cried out in pain, and the diesel fuel flowed around him. Someone pleaded with him to drag himself to safety, but it became obvious that he could not move. He had to have help.

The crowd of curious grew. They jostled for position and pressed closer to the accident scene, despite the potential for colossal tragedy should the fuel ignite.

Then Ken Bishop arrived.

When he saw that he could not drive around the accident scene, he stepped from his car and ran up the highway towards the crash site. At this time, he was acting more out of curiosity than concern because he could not yet see how serious things were. When he did manage to thread his way through the onlookers to the front of the crowd, he was appalled at what he saw. Several people were milling around, looking confused, but no one was going to the assistance of a man lying on the shoulder of the road. Then Bishop realized why.

A torrent of diesel fuel was washing down from one of the trucks into the north ditch. Already an ankle-deep lake of fuel lay between the injured man and safety. Bishop knew the fuel might explode at any second, yet he could not stand where he was and do nothing.

He had also recognized the man on the road! Because they shared the same occupation, Ken Bishop had seen Jim McAdie at truck stops and had occasionally had coffee with him.

"But even if I hadn't known him," Bishop recalls, "I knew I couldn't just stand there and let him die. I had to help."

Bishop yelled for the people to move back, and then sloshed through the pool of oil towards the spot where Jim McAdie lay in pain. Once he reached the trucker, he quickly placed a tourniquet on the injured man's leg, then raced around to the front of the transport to see if he could locate its driver. No one was visible, so Bishop frantically tore through the wreckage, silently hoping anyone in the cab would be alive.

At that point, a bystander lit a cigarette.

What McAdie remembers as "a big shot of fire" exploded around him. A column of burning oil shot into the sky and a boom like a thunderclap shook the ground. McAdie ducked his head, prayed as he had never prayed before, and prepared to die.

The shattering blast hit Ken Bishop with the impact of an express train. He was hurled into the air and thrown nine metres away, over McAdie into the deep snow near the railway. His oil-spattered clothes were burning, obscuring his vision and searing his hair and eyebrows.

Bishop immediately rolled around in the snow, doused the flames and looked for the man he wanted to save. Over by the trucks, McAdie screamed for help, his vision now obscured by dense black smoke that seemed to be everywhere. Yet he kept yelling, and Bishop prepared to do what he could to save the unfortunate driver. With his arm over his face in order to give himself some protection from the flames, he stumbled towards the spot where McAdie lay.

The roaring flames and smoke made it hard to see, but Bishop persevered. He eventually reached the injured trucker, and then, slowly, laboriously and painfully, managed to drag the man from danger. Bishop was now badly burned and virtually exhausted.

"All my clothes except my belt and my boots were burned off," he says. "I was barely alive."

Fifteen kilometres away, in Vegreville, the first call concerning the accident had already reached the Royal Canadian Mounted Police. "Due to the heavy traffic conditions, all available personnel were dispatched," recalls Clark Wolff, the police sergeant who headed the investigation into the accident. "Some officers were in uniform, others in civilian dress. The local fire department also responded."

At the scene itself, the plight of Bishop had not been eased. Despite his pleas for help to those who stood around, no one came forward to assist. His smouldering clothes were hanging from his frame and his face and hands were blackened from the fire. More than 40 percent of his body had been burned. Again and again he begged for help, until finally three women produced a blanket that he pulled around his shoulders.

Finally, exasperated and trembling with rage and pain, he made his way to his own car and managed to load McAdie into it for the trip to St. Joseph's General Hospital in Vegreville. Bishop had to do the driving himself, but before reaching the hospital he passed out. A second driver eventually completed the journey.

*   *   *

Ken Bishop spent 18 days in hospitals in Vegreville and Edmonton while his burns healed. He was off work for three years because he risked his life to save another human being from certain death. James McAdie recovered.

On April 5, 1976, Ken Bishop was awarded the Cross of Valour for the selfless courage of his daring rescue.

Sceviour, Miller and Fudge

The sea was calm at daybreak, but by noon the weather had closed in and the horizon had disappeared. Sheets of freezing rain, swept by a wild north wind, lashed the vessel, sending clouds of stinging spray across her decks and on into the chilling wastes of the North Atlantic. The ship strained in the storm. The screws plunged in the troughs between the waves, then screamed in the air when the stern was heaved above the surface. By 2:30 what little ceiling existed under the low clouds seemed to disappear and sky and water became as one, a boiling maelstrom that tossed the *Remoy* like a cork.

The Danish trawler had been in the area for days, fishing for shrimp along the northern coast of Labrador. Ordinarily, hundreds of islands, most of them barren rock, provided a measure of protection from the rolling sea, but on this Sunday, November 19, 1978, the frigid gales gave no quarter. The *Remoy* was in danger. Twenty-nine-year-old Captain Ulf Snarby knew it, and so did the crew of 11 who were with him.

He decided to head for port.

The journey was not easy. The roaring seas buffeted the *Remoy*, slammed against her hull and threatened to send her to a watery grave. At times, when her bow nosed downward into a long, rolling breaker, it seemed as if she would never right herself. Then slowly, fitfully, the bow would rise and a torrent of half-frozen slob ice would wash from the decks.

Each man on board, from the captain to the most inexperienced deckhand, respected the sea, understood its power, and braced himself against its every roll. At the same time, many fought down the queasiness and nausea that only those who have sailed rough seas can know.

In the wheelhouse, the strength of the storm was more obvious than elsewhere. Because it was above the rest of the ship, the wheelhouse moved farther with every roll. As well, the visibility here was normally better than at deck level, though during this November gale there was little that could be seen. The sea was just too rough, and the wind-driven rains obscured everything more than 100 metres away.

Because they knew they could not see anything if they went outside, most crew members found time to go to the galley. There they chatted about the storm, nursed cups of hot coffee and wondered how long it might take the *Remoy* to reach Nain, the little Labrador port where they would wait for better weather. Some felt they would be in harbour by nightfall; others believed the journey would take much longer than that. A few wondered if they would get there at all.

The storm was getting worse.

In the early afternoon, the shrieking winds occasionally abated, and when they did, the ocean seemed calmer. But with the approach of darkness, the wind picked up to 100 km/h, the temperature dropped to -25°C, and gusts of freezing rain and snow pelted the vessel.

The men in the galley braced themselves against the pitching of the ship and continued their small talk. But with each passing minute they found it harder and harder to think of anything but the storm. In the wheelhouse, the lurching motion of the *Remoy* was so violent no one could stand without support. A pair of binoculars placed on a shelf remained where they were for only a second before they crashed to the floor and slid across the room.

Ship navigation in the Labrador Sea is not easy at the best of times, but on this wild November afternoon it had become almost impossible. The charts on board all indicated water depth and safe channels, but the roaring seas made it harder and harder for the *Remoy* to stay on course. This was particularly true as Snarby headed into the long, winding Strathcona Run, the channel that led to Nain. Here, the hundreds of shoals and craggy islands and the pounding surf were a mariner's nightmare.

But Ulf Snarby had a more serious problem.

The waves that washed across the decks of the *Remoy* had become a matter of great concern. The sea ports at the stern of the ship, small doors that automatically opened and closed to let the water run off the deck, had frozen open. Sea water rushed in, and in the intense cold, froze on the deck and gradually became thicker and thicker. The ship began to list to port.

The list was barely noticeable at first, but soon became more and more pronounced. Snarby ordered his men to free the valves controlling the sea ports, but the task became impossible. Attempts to prop the ports shut did not work either. Each time a wave sloshed over the deck, the props were torn loose. In the meantime, the list increased.

The port side of the ship sank lower and lower in the water as the ice on the deck became heavier. Finally, Captain Snarby knew the *Remoy* would capsize unless something was done — and soon. He began to sail a sharp zigzag course in the hope that the wrenching of the ship from side to side might unclog the ports and enable some of the water on the stern section of the deck to drain. The manoeuvre failed.

Then, as he stood in the wheelhouse wondering what else he could do to remove the water from the deck, the radar screen in front of him suddenly went blank. The small engines that drove the scanners had frozen. By this time, night had come.

That was when Ulf Snarby decided to call for help.

While all this was happening, several other trawlers had successfully navigated the Strathcona Run and reached Nain. Two of these were the *Zaragoza* and the *Zermatt*. A 29-year-old named Martin Sceviour worked on the *Zaragoza*.

"When we heard Goose Bay radio issuing storm warnings, we headed for Nain," recalls Sceviour today. "Most of the shrimp fleet came in at this time. Then a number of us went to the Atsanik Lodge to wait until the weather got better.

"We had been fishing about 60 kilometres out of Nain, but by late that Sunday afternoon we had been in port for four hours or so. I was at the lodge when I heard about the *Remoy*. Apparently the RCMP picked up the distress call."

Only one ship, far out at sea, heard Ulf Snarby radio his SOS.

Fortunately, that vessel was able to contact a receiving station in Hopedale, a tiny Labrador community 150 kilometres south of Nain. But even though the message was now on the coast, transmission troubles caused a delay of two hours before the call for help got to Nain. As he attempted to reach Nain, the radio operator in Hopedale learned to his dismay that his base transmission tower had been flattened by the storm. Never-

The small port of Nain.

theless, the plea for assistance eventually got through.

"The RCMP came to the lodge and told us there was a ship in trouble," recounts Harold Miller, then 20, also with the *Zaragoza*. "The *Zermatt* went out to see what could be done. Neither Martin Sceviour nor I was on board at this time."

The RCMP loaned a motor boat to the *Zermatt* for the trip. The small outboard was hauled onto the trawler, and the rescue mission began. By this time, the problem-plagued *Remoy* was aground.

Once he found that his ship was on the verge of capsizing and his radar had gone, Ulf Snarby decided to take his ship in to the nearest island and deliberately force her aground. He reasoned that both he and his men would have a greater chance of survival if they were closer to land. But even though the *Remoy* came to rest on a sand bottom, the surf crashing on surrounding rocks would mean certain death to anyone foolhardy enough to try to paddle to shore. A rubber raft lowered into

Snarby forced his ship aground on this rugged coast to prevent it from capsizing.

the sea was swamped in seconds. The dingy was hauled back on board and the men of the ship settled down to wait for rescue.

The wait was long, tiresome, and at times seemingly hopeless.

It took the *Zermatt* about an hour and a half to reach the crippled *Remoy,* and when the rescuers saw where the 40-metre trawler was aground, they were amazed that she had not been torn apart among the rocks. Giant breakers broke over the grounded vessel, and the ice that coated her was thick, and getting heavier with every minute that passed. The sea was close to deck level on one side.

Captain Kirk Mitchell of the *Zermatt* took his ship close to the *Remoy* — too close. The tide in the area was dropping, and without warning, the *Zermatt* hit a sandbar and shuddered to a stop. Mitchell immediately ordered the engines reversed and the *Zermatt* slowly backed towards deeper water, 300 metres from shore.

Just then the emergency lights on the *Remoy* went out. The Danish trawler was now little more than an ice-coated hulk in the storm. But, hulk or not, there were still a dozen worried men on board.

Captain Mitchell again eased the 50-metre *Zermatt* as close as he dared to the *Remoy*. He also ordered a powerful searchlight on board his ship to be directed at the vessel on the rocks. Then, with the light as a kind of direction finder, men on the *Zermatt* fired rocket lines towards the *Remoy,* in the hope of rigging a line between the ships. The wild wind tossed the rockets into the sea. An attempt to launch a lifeboat was also unsuccessful. The little boat sank almost as soon as it hit the water. The time now was 11:30 P.M.

On the *Remoy,* the stranded fishermen watched each rescue attempt with heavy hearts, and despaired as each effort failed. They were now without light or heat; their stricken ship was almost covered with ice, and they knew that at any minute the pounding waves might tear their boat apart. If that happened, there would be no possible survival. No one could ever swim to shore. Not only was the sea violent, but the terrible cold would kill a man in minutes. Finally someone mentioned that the *Zermatt*'s lights seemed to be farther away.

Several men peered into the blackness and scoffed at the suggestion that the rescue boat had backed off. But the lights of the *Zermatt* did become fainter and finally disappeared entirely. The rescuers were gone!

Though the crew of the *Remoy* wondered if they had been abandoned, such was not the case. Kirk Mitchell had already sent a radio message to Nain, to the RCMP, asking them to locate another boat that could be launched from the *Zermatt*. Mitchell said he would be back in port in an hour and a half.

"When word got around that the first rescue was a failure — that they were going out again — Harold Miller and I volunteered to go," says Martin Sceviour. "The RCMP borrowed a boat from some of the Inuit in Nain, and Harold and I took it out to meet the *Zermatt*.

"This was a fibreglass speedboat, about six metres long. It had a little cabin in the middle, but you steered it at the back.

"We had no trouble getting it on board the *Zermatt,* but the trip back out to the *Remoy* took another hour and a half. As we were going out, I found myself wondering about the safety of the guys we were going to rescue — whether we would get to them before their boat sank or they froze to death."

The *Zermatt* anchored about a kilometre from the shoal where the *Remoy* lay. Between the ships the frightening gale blew the crests from wavetops, lashing with spray the men who struggled to drop the speedboat into the water. Even the *Zermatt,* which now carried some 23 men, lurched up and down like a rodeo rider on the back of a horse. The time was 2:00 A.M.

The speedboat was lowered over the side, and the harried efforts of the men seemed to be successful. No one smiled, but in the garish floodlights from the trawler, the rain-and-spray-drenched fishermen watched the little boat and held firmly to a line hooked to her bow. But just as Lester Fudge, the first mate of the *Zermatt* was about to go down into the outboard, a freezing breaker crashed against her and she filled with water.

"I really didn't think we would make it, when I saw the size of the wave that swamped the little boat," says Martin Sceviour. "We knew if we tried to sail in something that small we would have to bail nonstop."

As soon as they realized what had happened, the *Zermatt* crew hauled the speedboat back on board. The icy water was dumped out of it and the motor removed and hurriedly dried. Finally the little vessel was launched a second time, but with the line still hooked to the *Zermatt* in case the sea proved to be too rough. Lester Fudge, Martin Sceviour and Harold Miller all volunteered to attempt the rescue. Fudge drove the boat and Miller bailed water out of it, while Sceviour stood in front of the cabin, held on for dear life, and directed Fudge towards the *Remoy*. The wild ocean winds and the freezing spray made it impossible for Fudge to see much past the little cabin. From his position in the stern of the outboard, he yelled up to the *Zermatt* and told the crew to let the rope out slowly, in case the speedboat swamped.

"The three of us felt better because that line

was there," recalls Miller today. "But then something went wrong and they had to cut the rope. From then on we were left to look after ourselves. I remember being very tense as we started on that first trip over to the *Remoy*. I had to bail all the way."

In the outboard, the three men felt the seas were like mountains. Huge breakers rolled over the six-metre craft, tossed it towards the black and rainy sky, and then dropped it so far between the waves that every minute or so neither the *Remoy* nor the *Zermatt* could be seen. As well, the stinging lash of blowing wave crests soaked the men to the skin, despite the weatherproof slickers they wore. On all sides, floating masses of half-formed ice washed against the boat, hampered its progress and strained the already overworked motor.

But finally the rescuers reached the ice-covered *Remoy*.

As he drew in close to the stricken shrimp boat, Les Fudge decided to use the rubber raft from the *Remoy* as a kind of bumper. Once the dinghy was in position, Sceviour tossed a line towards the *Remoy*.

Almost as soon as the line was taut the *Remoy* crew prepared to abandon ship.

"We can't take you all at once," yelled Fudge. "We'll have to make two trips. Come on now, one at a time, jump!"

The first man clambered down to the speedboat. Six others followed in less than a minute.

"Okay, that's all for now," hollered Fudge. "We don't want to sink this thing. We'll be back."

With that, Sceviour pulled the line back in, Fudge reversed the motor and the tiny outboard backed out into the night. Harold Miller bailed for all he was worth.

The journey back to the *Zermatt* was worse than the trip out. With 10 men on board, the motor boat was precariously low in the water. Often the sea was only a few centimetres from the gunwales, and to Miller it seemed as if every second wave washed over them.

Yet somehow, after almost 40 minutes defying death from the elements, Fudge eased in beside the *Zermatt* and seven grateful men climbed on board. Fudge, Miller and Sceviour headed back into the storm.

An hour later they returned with the last of the men from the *Remoy*.

Captain Mitchell ordered the speedboat brought on board. Then he weighed anchor and headed for Nain. The rescue was completed — almost 11 hours after the *Remoy* ran aground.

*   *   *

After resting for a few hours, Lester Fudge, Martin Sceviour and Harold Miller helped chop ice from the trawlers. A day later, they all returned to sea. On April 6, 1981, all three stood in front of the Governor General of Canada to receive the Cross of Valour.

The *Remoy* was pumped out, hauled off the shoal and towed into port for repairs. She is again at sea.

René Jalbert

Just before 9:45 on the morning of May 8, 1984, a man dressed in military camouflage drove a beige Buick Skyhawk up to the south doors of the National Assembly building in Quebec City. He switched off the ignition, carefully adjusted the beret he was wearing, and reached across the seat for two 9mm sub-machine guns. He then stepped from the car, slung one weapon over his shoulder, cradled the other in his hands and walked to the side door.

At about the same time, journalists at radio station CJRP, some two kilometres away, were listening to a tape brought to them a few minutes earlier. The red-bearded man who delivered the recording had worn military fatigues and had a hunting knife dangling from his thigh. He told the woman who received the cassette not to play it until after 10:00 A.M. She passed the message to her boss, broadcaster André Arthur.

Even though Arthur was on the air at the time, he told his staff to listen to the tape right away. The appearance of the man who delivered it had been alarming.

The first five or six minutes on the cassette were a rambling commentary, in French, about the Parti Québécois and the failings of its language policies. But then the male voice turned to a more strident theme: "The government which presently is in office is going to be destroyed . . . I believe these are people who have done a lot of wrong, not only to the French language in Quebec, but in Canada. What I am doing isn't for me, but

for people in the future who speak the French language . . . There is no longer anyone who can stop me . . . I want to destroy the Parti Québécois."

The staff at CJRP had heard enough. André Arthur phoned the police. Unfortunately, the call came too late.

The man with the machine guns bounded up the five steps to the legislature doors. He pulled the right one open and stepped inside.

The receptionist on duty at the time was an attractive, outgoing young woman named Jacynthe Richard. She looked up as the man entered, smiled and started to say good morning to him. Her greeting became a scream.

The man swung the muzzle of one of the machine guns towards the receptionist, steadied himself for a fraction of a second and squeezed the trigger.

A volley of shots echoed across the hall and reverberated down the marble corridors of the government building. Several bullets tore into Richard's right arm and chest and knocked her backwards towards the door of an adjoining office. As she fell, the gunman pointed his firearm at a red emergency telephone nearby. He fired a single burst from the weapon and the telephone disintegrated. He then turned away from the critically wounded Richard and began walking to the right, down a corridor that runs parallel to Grand Allée, Quebec City's best known street.

As he went, the gunman continued to shoot — at the floor, the walls, the ceiling, and anyone who moved. Some time after the affair, when I was researching this book, I saw bullet holes the size of silver dollars in the marble walls that line the route of the rampage. Even a casual glance at the wreckage indicates that the man responsible was a man out of control.

When he came to the end of the first corridor, the gunman turned to his left and moved towards the main doors of the Parliament. Coming towards him was security guard Denis Samson, who had been in the front lobby when the firing started. Samson was on his way to see what was happening.

He did not get far.

The gunman shot the guard in the abdomen and Samson crumpled. Then the intruder headed for the staircase leading to the Blue Room, the ornate Legislative Chamber that is the Quebec National Assembly. It was here that he expected to find the objects of his quest.

While the vicious onslaught was underway in the Parliament buildings, a 63-year-old ex-soldier named René Jalbert was driving the two kilometres from his home to his office in the National Assembly building. Major Jalbert had been a member of the famed French Canadian Royal 22nd Regiment, often called the Van Doos, and was a veteran of the Second World War and Korea. On May 8, 1984, he was the sergeant-at-arms at the National Assembly, and in that role was responsible for the security of the place. On this day he would prove himself worthy of his calling.

Jalbert had the radio on in his car, but his

mind was not on the music. That morning at 10:00 a parliamentary committee was meeting in the Blue Room, and before the meeting began Jalbert wanted to be sure everything was ready.

Directly across Grand Allée from the National Assembly is a large cement and glass office building locally known as H Block, or "The Bunker," where government officials have their offices. Under the building is a reserved parking area. On that cold, rainy Tuesday morning Jalbert was happy to be able to leave his car indoors.

The sergeant-at-arms parked, locked his car and walked through a tunnel under Grand Allée towards his office on the basement level of the National Assembly building. He wore a light beige trenchcoat over a dark suit and carried a briefcase. Just as he emerged from the tunnel he was told that someone was shooting upstairs.

By this time the gunman was two floors above, in the Legislative Chamber itself.

He had rushed past the wounded security guard and up the stairs towards the mezzanine level of the building where the parliamentary restaurant is situated. Fortunately, he did not realize that several members of the National Assembly — his intended targets — were in the restaurant at the time. He was too busy firing his machine gun at the carpet, at the stairs, at the walls, and at 54-year-old Camille Lepage, a parliamentary messenger who happened to be descending the stairs at the time. Lepage, an unmarried former farmer from the Ile d'Orleans, died quickly.

Inside the restaurant, Finance Minister

Jacques Parizeau and others were having break-fast. When the sound of gunfire was heard in the lobby below, someone quickly closed the restaurant doors, but bullets crashed through them. One nicked the desk where the cash register sat, although no one in the room was injured. The man with the gun continued up the stairs. "I have a gang to kill on the third floor," he shouted.

There is a large, carpeted landing on the top floor of the building. To the gunman's left was the Legislative Chamber, the Blue Room, while to the right was the Red Room, the Assembly's old Council Chamber. In the Red Room at the time were groups of school children touring the building. When they heard the gunfire on the stairs, guides and teachers quickly ordered the youngsters to lie on the floor, and the doors to the room were closed. The gunman turned to his left on the landing and stormed into the Blue Room across the hall. Later, all the students were safely evacuated.

The gunman knew that his moment of triumph was at hand. Now he would come face to face with the members of the National Assembly, the majority of them men and women of the Parti Québécois, who he believed were doing wrong to the French-speaking populace of Quebec and of Canada as a whole. Now he would somehow right those wrongs. Now he would show the world that one man alone could make his mark, could make a difference.

But the chamber was almost empty.

"Où sont les députés? Je vais les tuer! (Where are the legislators? I am going to kill them!)" the gunman screamed. "Where have they all gone? I am going to bring down this government. I am going to rid the province of this government. I don't see them," he wailed.

The man looked around the room, an expression of disappointment on his face. Then he began blasting away with a machine gun, "left and right, up and down, everywhere," according to a man who was there at the time. A few civil servants and others were present, preparing the room for the coming meeting. Some of these were pages who were filling water glasses and distributing writing materials. One of them was Georges Boyer, 59, a former military policeman in the Canadian Forces, and since 1980 an Assembly employee. He was shot in the legs but managed to crawl behind a press table at the rear of the room. He lay there for over an hour and lost so much blood that he died later in the day.

Another visitor was Roger Lefrançois, who worked for Quebec's office of the director of elections. He and a colleague had just entered the Blue Room as the gunman arrived. The 57-year-old Lefrançois looked around to see what was happening when he was splattered by a volley of shells from point-blank range. His body jerked backwards, his glasses flew off and blood poured from his mouth. He died where he fell.

Rejean Dionne was a 32-year-old cameraman in the National Assembly. He heard the gunman enter the Chamber, but quickly dropped to the floor and lay motionless between the desks of René Levesque and Social Affairs Minister Camille

Laurin. But even though he felt no pain at first, Dionne later realized he had been shot in the right elbow. Others were wounded as well, but had flattened themselves on the floor behind desks, hardly daring to breathe.

Louise d'Allair was one of several people waiting for the committee meeting to begin. D'Allair later related how the gunman suddenly appeared in the doorway of the room, pointed a weapon at her as he changed an ammunition clip, then moved the muzzle away from her and shot at others in the group. "I saw the bullets hit," she recalls. "I saw blood on the floor and I realized one of my colleagues had been hit." She dropped to the floor herself and took cover behind a small table.

When he failed to find his intended quarry, the agitated gunman stormed the length of the room and shot at everything in sight, including four of the five wall-mounted television cameras used to film debates in the Chamber. He then walked past the desk used by René Levesque, past the Speaker's chair at the front of the room, and out into a small lobby adjacent to the Chamber. The lobby opens in turn into a hallway where there is an elevator leading to the lower floors.

He walked to the elevator, sprayed the control buttons and the stainless steel door with bursts from one of his guns and shot several rounds down the hall, into the walls, floors and ceiling. He then turned and headed back to the Blue Room.

By the time the terrified occupants of the smoke-filled lobby dared look up, the gunman had returned to the Blue Room, walked up the three steps to the Speaker's platform and ensconced himself in the Speaker's chair. As he settled back and surveyed the historic Chamber in front of him, he brought one of the machine guns up to chest level and began firing everywhere.

"I heard a burst of fire from an automatic weapon as I stepped off the elevator," recalls René Jalbert, who had arrived to investigate the shooting. "There were a lot of 9mm shells lying around in the small lobby just behind the Chamber, so I knew it had to be a machine gun of some kind. I decided to be careful and to go very slowly."

Jalbert picked his way through the shells and the debris that had fallen from the walls and ceiling and cautiously made his way to the Blue Room. He entered the Chamber through the same door the gunman had used a moment or so earlier.

"When I looked around from behind the Speaker's chair, I could see the length of the room," says Jalbert, "and I could see where the fellow was firing. Mr. Levesque's desk was to my right, and a television camera was above it and slightly to the rear. The guy was spraying that side of the room with bullets, and I could see both the wood on Mr. Levesque's desk and the plaster on the right wall exploding. If the Premier or any of the other députés had been there, they would have died for sure. I also noticed a strong smell of gunpowder in the air."

Finally there was silence and Jalbert made his move.

"Stop firing," yelled the sergeant-at-arms. "Somebody is coming in to talk to you."

Denis Lortie.

René Jalbert stands beside the Speaker's chair in the Quebec National Assembly.

"I then peeked around from behind the Speaker's chair and I yelled again, in French, 'Stop, I want to talk to you!' I looked at him and he looked at me, and he said 'Yes' and he did stop," recalls Jalbert.

"I didn't wait. I just carried on, and I stood beside a little table that was next to the Speaker's chair, where the guy was sitting. 'What are you doing here?' I asked. 'Don't you see that this room has all been recently renovated and it's beautiful. You're wrecking everything. Why are you doing this? You're a taxpayer and I'm a taxpayer. This is costing us money.' "

The gunman gaped at Jalbert. The sergeant-at-arms continued. "I see you are a soldier. I'm a soldier too — at least I'm a veteran. If you allow me, if you promise not to shoot, I'll take my wallet out and I'll show you my discharge card."

During this interlude, the man in the Speaker's chair was obviously nervous. His face was pale and he was perspiring heavily. At times he seemed to have trouble getting his breath. The gun in his hand was waving around and pointed at Jalbert. The sergeant-at-arms went on.

"I didn't want him to think I was pulling a gun," explains Jalbert, in recalling the incident. "I told him he could look at my card, so I slowly reached for my wallet. He hesitated and finally agreed to let me. I handed him my card and he looked at it, back and front, for about 30 seconds or so. Then he handed it back and I put it away.

"I did everything slowly because I didn't want him to explode. He was terribly nervous and the gun was waving around, still pointed at me. But I still didn't know who he was."

"Look," Jalbert said to the gunman, "I told you I was a soldier and I proved it to you. I showed you my card. Now I see that you are a soldier, or at least you are dressed like a soldier, but I'm not sure if you really are one. Have you some identification?"

"Yes," answered the gunman and he handed Jalbert a card from his pocket. The inscription read: LORTIE, DENIS — CORPORAL. The date of birth indicated that the man was 25.

"From then on, I called him either 'Denis' or 'Corporal,'" says Jalbert. "And I kept on talking and asking him questions because I wanted to calm him down and get his mind off that machine gun. I didn't want to get shot."

"Denis," said Jalbert to the gunman, "do you smoke? I would like a cigarette and I'll give you one."

Lortie said he did not smoke.

"Then I want a smoke," said Jalbert. "Do you mind if I smoke?"

Lortie replied that he did not mind, so Jalbert lit the first of almost two packs of Matinée cigarettes he would smoke in the next four hours.

"Well, if you don't smoke," the sergeant-at-arms asked the gunman, "what do you do? Do you take drugs or something?"

"My drug is gum," answered Lortie.

"What kind of gum?" Jalbert wondered.

"Dentine. It helps increase the saliva in my mouth," Lortie explained.

Corporal Lortie was chewing gum at the time, so Jalbert suggested he chew another piece — anything to calm the young man down. But instead of doing as Jalbert wanted, Lortie reached into his mouth, took out his false teeth and threw them on the floor. Then he took off his beret and flung it over a microphone in front of the Speaker's chair. Jalbert did not react. Instead, he asked the gunman why he was doing all the shooting.

"I knew he had some kind of problem," Jalbert recalls, "and I told him we should get out of the Chamber so we could talk. I told him I was there to help him. What I did not say was that I was afraid some of the people who were supposed to be coming to the 10 o'clock meeting would show up and he would kill them. I later heard about the school children who were on the floor in the Red Room. I know now if they had started to come out, Lortie would have shot them. At this stage, I did not know that he had murdered three people and injured 13 others. I didn't even know some were in the Chamber. I saw no one when I entered."

The others in the room were hiding behind desks and remaining perfectly still. Later one of them recalled what the ordeal was like for her: "I was terrified all the time I was there. At first I thought I was the only one alive," she added. "I couldn't hear a thing.

"Then I heard Mr. Jalbert and I said to myself: 'Merci, mon Dieu.' (Thank You, my God.)"

At least one other person knew what was happening in the Blue Room. Johanne Tanguay was in another area of the building, but it was she who operated the only television camera that had not been wrecked by gunfire. The camera was run by remote control, and it gave Tanguay a view from the gallery above the floor of the house. The entire interchange between Lortie and Jalbert in the Legislature was videotaped. "From time to time, Lortie took shots at my camera," she recalls, "so I stopped moving it to record what was happening."

She filmed Jalbert in his conversation with Lortie, but she also noticed a movement that Jalbert explains: "Out of the corner of my eye I saw a flash of blonde hair behind one of the desks," says the sergeant-at-arms. "It was one of the pages. I motioned her to stay down and then I started to negotiate for the release of everyone in the room, but I still didn't know who was there. I asked Lortie."

"Yes," he said, "there are some there, and there, and there," and he pointed to different areas in the room.

"Look," Jalbert said to the gunman, "we are discussing your problem here, because I want to help you. But we should be discussing it alone. If there are people here, you have to promise to let them go out safely. Then, when we are alone, we can talk."

After much hesitation, Lortie consented and those who were hiding in the chamber walked out, some of them bleeding. Once they were apparently alone, Jalbert and Lortie continued to talk for almost 40 minutes. At one stage, Jalbert noticed a security guard in the gallery at the opposite end of the chamber. He called to the guard and ordered two cups of coffee. When the coffee arrived, Jalbert gave a cup to the killer and drank the other himself. Gradually, the gunman was becoming calmer.

"As we were having coffee, I asked Lortie if he realized there might be policemen in the gallery who would shoot him," Jalbert recalls.

"Oh, that's all right. I couldn't care less," Lortie answered.

Jalbert later admitted that the reply chilled him. "I knew then that he was prepared to die, that he expected to die, but I had no intention of dying with him, so I knew we had to get out of there. I tried again to talk him into going to my office."

This time, Jalbert got his wish.

Lortie got up, picked up his guns and followed the sergeant-at-arms from the room. And even though the man behind him was a killer and held a gun to his back, Jalbert never flinched. He led Denis Lortie to the elevator, and after some difficulty getting it to work because it had been shot up earlier, managed to open the door and ride to the basement.

"Once we got there, we went right to my office," says René Jalbert.

Lucienne Lebel, Jalbert's secretary, was on the phone when the two men arrived. The police had called her earlier and asked her to remain in her office and to lock the door. When she heard Jalbert coming in she felt relieved, knowing that only he and the cleaning staff had office keys. As

Jalbert and Lortie entered, she walked towards them.

"Corporal Lortie, I would like you to meet my secretary, Madame Lebel," said Jalbert, in an attempt to let the killer know that all was well. "Madame Lebel, Corporal Lortie."

Lortie shook Lebel's hand and kissed her on the cheek. She smiled at him, thankful that the long, violent nightmare was finally over. Her boss was safe at last, and this polite young man with him must be a member of the police SWAT team, which she knew was somewhere in the building.

In her happiness at seeing René Jalbert and the man she believed was a policeman, Lucienne Lebel accidently knocked over a small flower vase on her desk. When she reached for some tissues to sponge up the water, Lortie smiled and assisted her. Then Jalbert invited the corporal to sit down.

"May I talk to my secretary, Denis?" Jalbert asked.

"Yes, of course," Lortie responded.

"Madame Lebel," said Jalbert, "go up to the restaurant and get a cup of coffee."

"But Mr. Jalbert, the restaurant will be closed now," she answered, "and I really don't need a cup of coffee."

"Madame Lebel," snapped the sergeant-at-arms with feigned harshness, *"Go and get a cup of coffee!* I want to talk to Corporal Lortie *alone*."

The bewildered Lebel frowned at her boss and left the office. As soon as she was outside the door, SWAT team members told her who Lortie was and whisked her away. She was aghast at what had just transpired.

Jalbert had decided at this point that if Lortie became violent again only two people would die: Jalbert himself, murdered by the corporal, and Lortie, by suicide. The fact that Madame Lebel was safe was a relief.

"Because we were alone, and Lortie had no one to perform for, I felt I might convince him to surrender," explains René Jalbert today. "If he shot me that was better than taking the chance of letting him shoot a lot of other people. I decided to keep talking. He was sitting on a chair, across the desk from me."

"Denis," he said, "you have two hands and two weapons. Why don't you pull another chair up beside you and you can put one of your machine guns on it. Then you can put the other one on the desk in front of you and it will be handy if you need it. That way you will have both hands free and we can talk."

Lortie did as Jalbert suggested.

Major Jalbert then began a long, wide-ranging discussion with the murderer in front of him. The topics they covered ranged from why Lortie did what he did, to army life, to his own upbringing, to politics, travel and sports. Reflecting back on the almost four hours of conversation, Jalbert now recalls that Lortie was only able to give a rather jumbled set of reasons for his actions — the same reasons that were set out in the tape delivered to the radio station earlier in the day. As he talked, the corporal began to relax as Jalbert gained his trust.

Then the phone rang.

Lortie jumped, put his hand on a gun and glared at Jalbert.

"May I answer the phone?" the major asked.

"Yes," the corporal agreed.

The caller was Jalbert's wife Nanette. She was phoning from work because she had heard rumours of trouble at the National Assembly. At this point she had no idea that her husband was in any way involved, much less that he was staring down the barrel of a 9mm sub-machine gun.

"Are you all right, René? What's going on?"

"Nothing is going on now, dear," answered her husband. "There was a bit of trouble a while ago, but I'm a little busy right now. I can't talk to you. I'll call you back."

"Okay," answered Nanette Jalbert, and she hung up.

The gunman relaxed and the conversation between the killer and the sergeant-at-arms continued.

Then the telephone jangled a second time.

Lortie flinched and pulled a loaded pistol from his belt. He pulled the hammer back, set the weapon on the desk in front of him and watched to see what Jalbert would do.

"May I answer the phone, Denis?" the major asked.

"Yes," answered Corporal Lortie.

The second caller was a journalist. Jalbert

talked for a moment and hung up. After that, several reporters called, and each time the telephone rang, Lortie became more and more upset.

"The calls from the journalists were really bothering me," admits Jalbert today. "There were so many that I had to start hanging up on them just to stop the ringing. I could see that Lortie was getting worked up, and the phone was making what I was trying to do more difficult. I would get him calmed down, the phone would ring and I would have to start all over again. Finally I convinced him that what he had in mind was impossible, that he should surrender."

"There's no way!" Lortie retorted vehemently. "I won't surrender to the Quebec police. I want to be treated humanely."

Jalbert was not sure what this comment meant. But when he heard it, he tried another approach.

"Look, you're a soldier, I'm a soldier. If you agree, I will arrange for you to surrender to the military police. I know they will treat you fairly." Lortie was unmoved, and Jalbert recalls that he must have made the suggestion at least 20 times. He also pointed out to the killer that he could not stay where he was forever. Finally the words that Jalbert longed to hear were spoken.

"Okay, I'll surrender."

Jalbert immediately telephoned his friend Colonel Armand Roy at nearby Canadian Forces Base Valcartier. The sergeant-at-arms began to explain his predicament when Roy interrupted.

"Yes, René, I know. I'm listening to the radio here. Can I help you?"

Jalbert asked Roy to send two military police officers to the Assembly building because Corporal Lortie had agreed to surrender to them. Roy said they would be there in half an hour.

"Corporal," Jalbert said to Lortie, "do you want to talk to Colonel Roy? Then you will know I've been telling you the truth. He is going to send the military police."

Lortie nodded, picked up his pistol in one hand and the phone in the other and talked to Armand Roy. The conversation lasted about two minutes, after which Jalbert noticed that Lortie had visibly relaxed. The killer sat down, placed the revolver on the desk in front of him and looked at Jalbert.

"Denis," said Jalbert, "it's almost noon and I'm hungry. Are you hungry?"

"No," responded Lortie.

"Well, even if you're not," Jalbert went on, "I am. I'm going to order some sandwiches and coffee for us."

Lortie didn't say anything.

Jalbert picked up the telephone and called the Office of Security for the building. A SWAT team member answered and the sergeant-at-arms ordered sandwiches for two. Fifteen minutes later the food was delivered in a paper bag and placed on the floor in the corridor, about eight metres from Jalbert's office.

Major Jalbert opened the door to the hall, and with Lortie standing just inside, walked slowly to the sandwiches and picked up the bag. All the way, the young killer had one of his machine guns trained on Jalbert's back. Jalbert returned and Lortie locked the office door. The bag was opened and both men had lunch.

"As I was going for the sandwiches, I didn't know whether he would shoot me in the back or not," winces Jalbert as he recalls the incident. "I saw two SWAT guys in the corridor, but I knew I would be dead before they could take Lortie. At that time, I was afraid."

After they had eaten, the sergeant-at-arms asked Lortie why he had done what he had done, why he had done such a stupid thing. The young soldier started to cry.

"He cried for two or three minutes," said Jalbert, "and then he felt better. I knew then that he was back to normal. All morning I had been trying to establish a relationship of confidence between us, and I now knew I was getting somewhere. I pointed out to him that he had agreed to surrender to the military police, and that it was time we set forth the type of protocol that would be expected."

Jalbert then talked to Lortie as a soldier. "You are a corporal. I am a major. From now on, you will address me as Major and I will address you as Corporal. Is that understood?"

"Yes, Major!" Lortie barked.

"Well then," stated Jalbert, "we will now arrange for your surrender."

Half an hour later, Corporal Denis Lortie was in custody.

*   *   *

The murder trial of Denis Lortie, soldier, opened in Quebec City on January 7, 1985. The conviction on three charges of first degree murder of Denis Lortie, killer, came on February 13, 1985. The seven women and five men of the jury nodded assent when Quebec Superior Court Judge Ivan Mignault sentenced the young father of two to life imprisonment, without parole for 25 years.

At 11:00 A.M. on Friday, November 9, 1984, the first female governor general of Canada, Her Excellency Jeanne Sauvé, conferred the Cross of Valour on Major René M. Jalbert. Then the sergeant-at-arms flew back to Quebec to continue overseeing security at the National Assembly.

Achevé   Imprimerie
d'imprimer Gagné Ltée
au Canada Louiseville